North Carolina Barbecue

FLAVORED BY TIME

North Carolina Barbecue
FLAVORED BY TIME

Bob Garner

John F. Blair, Publisher   Winston-Salem, North Carolina

Second printing, 1996

The paper in this book meets the guidelines for permanence and durability of the Committee on Production Guidelines for Book Longevity of the Council on Library Resources.

Library of Congress Cataloging-in-Publication Data

Garner, Bob, 1946–
    North Carolina barbecue : flavored by time / Bob Garner.
         p.   cm.
    Includes index.
    ISBN 0-89587-152-1 (alk. paper)
    1. Barbecue cookery—North Carolina. 2. Restaurants—North Carolina—Guidebooks. I. Title.
TX840.B3G365 1996
641.7'6—dc20   96–22503

DESIGN BY DEBRA LONG HAMPTON

PRINTED AND BOUND BY R. R. DONNELLEY & SONS

FOR BOB AND TAD

Table of Contents

Acknowledgments ▪▪▪▪

I want to express my sincere appreciation to the many people who helped make this book possible.

I am indebted to Scott Moore-Davis, executive producer of UNC-TV's *North Carolina Now*, who first suggested that I do a series of segments on North Carolina barbecue restaurants, and to the rest of the management and staff at UNC-TV, whose enthusiasm and support for those broadcast segments ultimately led to my decision to write the book.

A special word of thanks goes to Jeff Hicks of the North Carolina Collection, UNC Library at Chapel Hill, whose early assistance in the research process was invaluable. I also very much appreciate the efforts and enthusiasm of Steve Massengill and Earl Ijames of the North Carolina Division of Archives and History, who helped me locate many of the book's historic photographs. Kay Saintsing of the Lexington Barbecue Festival also provided valuable assistance in this area.

I want to thank Keith Stamey of Stamey's Barbecue in Greensboro for his help at many different points—and for his peach cobbler.

I'm grateful to my brother-in-law, Tad Everett, for his help with recipes; to his wife Jayne for her hospitality; and to Bob and Beverly Everett for making their house and grounds available for any and all purposes.

Sincere thanks go to my editor, Andrew Waters, for his many insightful suggestions and for his patience.

To the congregation at Christ Church in Burlington: Thank you so much for your prayers and encouragement.

Finally, I extend my deepest appreciation to my lovely wife Ruthie, who served cheerfully and well as a researcher and assistant; and to Anna Barrett, Van, Nelson, and Everett for their belief in me and their constant support.

Introduction ▪▪▪

What is it about barbecue that makes it even more enjoyable to talk about than it is to eat—especially here in North Carolina?

For one thing, remembrances associated with barbecue connect us to a three-hundred-year heritage, both real and romanticized. Since the dawn of the automobile era, opinions about who prepared the best barbecue, like political attitudes, have been a legacy handed down solemnly from one generation to the next in the small towns and farming hamlets of eastern and piedmont North Carolina. (For some reason, the mountain area has never enjoyed much of a barbecue tradition.) In earlier days, the names of pioneering barbecue restaurateurs were spoken in reverent tones, usually by the males of the family, and the infrequent meal at one of those hallowed establishments was something like worshipping in church, as eyes closed and heads shook slowly and wordlessly back and forth over the evidence of grace bestowed in the form of peppery, chopped pork. In the intervals between such rites, frequent reminiscing no doubt elevated the quality of the barbecue to mythical proportions.

The renewed availability of cars and fuel at the end of World War II made searching for the best barbecue something of a pastime, and it quickly became a popular topic of conversation for returning servicemen and their families. Another new phenomenon, the drive-in restaurant, made sampling and comparison easy, and joint-hopping patrons soon were served thousands of warm, moist, coleslaw-crowned barbecue sandwiches, wrapped in waxed paper and brought outside on trays that clamped onto car windows.

But barbecue and its discourse take us back even further. Wispy, blue smoke floating above a coppery brown split pig, hissing and crackling over winking coals, drifts back across many generations of small farmers, sharecroppers, merchants, and traders, finally reaching the native inhabitants of northeastern North Carolina and tidewater Virginia, who almost certainly passed along the art of barbecuing to the settlers. It quickly spread throughout the region, but in the aristocracies of those "mountains of conceit," Virginia and South Carolina, barbecuing was often relegated to slaves, its secrets somewhat beneath the notice of polite society. However, within North Carolina's "vale of humility," barbecuing was, with a few exceptions, the occupation of farmers and journeymen, white and black, and its arts, methods, and mysteries were endlessly discussed and debated. That tradition has remained, and today, North Carolinians who

barbecue for a hobby or profitable sideline—and there are thousands of them—would list conversation and comparing notes at dozens of festivals and "cook-offs" at the top of their lists of reasons for practicing their hot, smoky art.

And there is a bottomless saucepot of esoterica and detail to be enjoyed by North Carolina barbecue buffs, just as there is among those who engage in the strange barbecue practices of other states. As food writer Craig Claiborne noted in the *New York Times*, "Differences center on the type of meat used (pork, beef or poultry) or its cut (pork shoulders, spareribs, or whole pig); the sauce (tomato based or vinegar with spices); the accompaniments (should coleslaw be tossed with mayonnaise or barbecue sauce?); or which woods impart the best flavor (hickory and/or oak or, more recently, mesquite). Should you baste or not? How do you prefer the meat: chopped, sliced, in chunks? In a sandwich or on a tray?"

There are other differences Claiborne didn't tackle: Is your pit open or enclosed with a chimney? How far do you place the meat above the coals? Do you cover the meat while it's cooking (to keep ashes from settling on it) or leave it uncovered? Once the meat is cooked, do you leave it on the fire overnight to impart more wood flavor? How finely do you chop the meat? . . . And do you do it by hand, with a cleaver, or by machine?

NORTH CAROLINA BARBECUE : *Flavored by Time*

And then there's the great North Carolina barbecue schism between east and west. No one quite knows why two distinct barbecue styles developed in North Carolina: whole-hog in the coastal plain, shoulders-only in the piedmont. But that distinction, together with the differences between eastern and western sauces and the regional variations in what's considered an appropriate barbecue side dish, has provided grist for an endlessly revolving mill of barbecue debate. It has also given North Carolina something of an undeserved national reputation for barbecue schizophrenia that, to outsiders, sullies the state's claim to have the best barbecue on the planet. The *New Yorker*'s Calvin Trillin wrote in his book *Alice, Let's Eat* of being "subjected to stern geographical probings" when he mentioned to former North Carolina residents that he had sampled barbecue in their home state. And in *Southern Food*, John Egerton sniffs, "There are two basic styles of North Carolina barbecue, and proponents of each are so disdainful of the other that doubt is cast on both."

But if the east-west controversy complicates our sales pitch to the outside world, it certainly makes life more interesting at home. If the truth were known, many of those hurling scorn and abuse at their barbecue cousins on the opposite side of Raleigh simply know how to get the most fun out of an argument and are playing a mischievous family

tussle for all it's worth. Newspaper, magazine, and television reporters, including this one, are notorious for keeping the argument going long after everyone else is ready to drop it. Sometimes there's even *intra*regional warfare. In the 1950s, Vernon Sechriest, who was then editor of the *Rocky Mount Evening Telegram* and Henry Belk, then editor of *The News-Argus* in Goldsboro started up a friendly rivalry over which of their respective cities served the best barbecue. "No self-respecting pig would wind up as a morsel of vinegar-tainted, half-burned nonsense as that served in Goldsboro," wrote Sechriest, while Belk was content to reply smugly that Rocky Mount barbecue "has some resemblance to mush." The mock debate grew so fierce that the Associated Press, deciding to milk the story a while longer, sent it out over the state wires.

Most of the millions of words written about North Carolina barbecue, however, have revolved around the contest for barbecue supremacy between east and west. Author and publisher Jerry Bledsoe, for years a columnist for the former *Greensboro Daily News*, carried on a long-running battle with Dennis Rogers of the *News and Observer*. Each regularly insisted—tongue firmly planted in cheek—that what passed for barbecue in the other's home region was actually nearly unfit for human consumption. "In the East, you get all these little things in your mouth and wonder what the hell they are," Bledsoe jeered. "They're ground-up skin. That's the only way they have to give the meat any flavor. So what you're getting is roast pork and ground skin with a little vinegar and hot peppers and salt on it." Rogers, taking aim at the piedmont custom of offering sliced as well as chopped barbecue, answered, "When I am hankering for a big piece of dead hog meat with tomato sauce, I like to follow the advice of my good friend Jerry Bledsoe and head west, where you find lots of it. For some silly reason, Jerry calls that barbecue."

Politicians probably love talking barbecue even more than writers because they feel it's a good way to connect with voters in terms of shared experience. Discussing the finer points of 'cue or tearing off a slab of meat at a pig picking gives a high-born candidate just the right hint of the common touch, while an office seeker from humbler circumstances can proudly out-redneck everyone on the subject.

Barbecue probably became inescapably linked to politics in the late '30s and early '40s, the heyday of the "political caravan"— a gaggle of campaigning politicians traveling in cars and buses. The caravans would pull into a town for a series of speeches, followed by a barbecue feed and handshaking. Thad Eure, who served as North Carolina's secretary of state for some sixty years and who called himself "the oldest rat in the Demo-cratic barn," recalled: "They'd advertise barbecue so much that whenever the caravan would move down the highways and roads in the state, all the pigs and hogs would see them coming and get out of the way."

While barbecue serves a useful political purpose, it can also be taxing on the body and soul over the length of a campaign. Rufus Edmisten (a mountaineer) admits his 1984 campaign for governor began to skid after he was overheard calling barbecue, "that damnable stuff." Some thirty years earlier, Herbert O'Keefe, a former editor of the *Raleigh Times*, had warned, "No man has ever been elected governor of North Carolina without eating more barbecue than was good for him." But once they're elected, the state's politicians— in Washington or in Raleigh—like nothing better than showing off the delights of their district by hosting a barbecue meal for their colleagues, often forging alliances or resolving differences over barbecue, slaw, and hush puppies or corn sticks brought in for the occasion from some big-name local restaurant. In honor of a similar type of political and social event that's extremely popular in our state, former governor Bob Scott was moved in 1972 to proclaim North Carolina "the pig pickin' capital of the world."

But the main reason we seldom tire of talking about barbecue is that it represents one of the few remaining antidotes to the mind-numbing homogeneity of the chain restau-

NORTH CAROLINA BARBECUE : *Flavored by Time*

rants and fast-food joints that sucks the color from our travel today. Nothing comes closer to reflecting local character than a good barbecue place—or at least that is what we would like to believe. In any case, whether we prefer to search for it off the beaten track or carefully choose it because of its longstanding reputation, enthusing about "that great barbecue place" is one of the honest pleasures of life in North Carolina.

For most of us, the tongue fails when it comes to expressing the delights—and the significance—of barbecue. But oh, what might we say if *we* were poets like eastern North Carolina native James Applewhite?

Barbecue Service

I have sought the elusive aroma
Around outlying cornfields, turned corners
Near the site of a Civil War surrender.
The transformation may take place
At a pit no wider than a grave,
Behind a single family's barn.
Those weathered ministers

Preside with the simplest of elements;
Vinegar and pepper, split pig and fire.
Underneath a glistening mountain in air,
Something is converted to a savor: the pig
Flesh purified by far atmosphere.
Like the slick-sided sensation from last
  summer,
A fish pulled quick from a creek
By a boy. Like breasts in a motel
With whiskey and twilight
Now a blue smoke in memory.
This smolder draws the soul of our longings.

I want to see all the old home folks,
Ones who may not last another year.
We will rock on porches like chapels
And not say anything, their faces
Impenetrable as different barks of trees.
After the brother who drank has been buried,
The graveplot stunned by sun
In the woods,
We men still living pass the bottle.
We barbecue pigs.
The tin-roofed sheds with embers
Are smoking their blue sacrifice
Across Carolina.

North Carolina Barbecue

FLAVORED BY TIME

Barbecue: the staple food of North Carolina political rallies
Courtesy North Carolina Division of Archives and History

A Three-Hundred-Year Tradition

▞▞▞▞ Lovers of genuine North Carolina barbecue sometimes complain, with a slight touch of superiority, that there are those outside the borders of the state who don't seem to understand—as all true Tar Heels do—that the word *barbecue* refers to what is produced on a rack above a bed of coals, and not the cooking apparatus itself. Someone from New York might say, for example, "Let's cook hot dogs and hamburgers on the barbecue." Even further afield, Australian actor Paul Hogan became a familiar face to American television viewers even before he starred in the *Crocodile Dundee* films when he appeared in tourism commercials promising prospective visitors that their Australian hosts would "put an extra shrimp on the 'barbie.'"

Sorry, folks, it looks like the Yankees and the Aussies have us on this one. The staid, old *Oxford English Dictionary* tells us our beloved *b* word comes from the Spanish *barbacoa*. The word originated in the seventeenth century on the island of Hispanola and was used to describe "a framework of sticks set upon posts," before quickly broadening into a verb to describe the process of cooking on such a framework. Barbecuing was evidently well established among the Indians of the Caribbean because a 1661 book describing Jamaica mentioned native inhabitants who hunted wild game "and their flesh forthwith Barbacu'd and eat."

(Note: Scholars have ridiculed the notion that the word *barbecue* comes from the French expression *barbe à queue*, meaning "beard to tail," saying it's a trivial conjecture suggested merely by the sound of the phrase. But don't tell that to old barbecue hands like Walter B. "Pete" Jones of the Skylight Inn in Ayden, who claims his family has been serving the specialty for 165 years. Pete is a staunch advocate of whole-hog barbecue who insists, "Your old word is, the barb's the snout and the tail's the *q*, which means you don't really have barbecue unless you have the whole pig cooked over wood coals—barb to *q*." Perhaps early colonists noticed the similarity between the terms and began using them interchangeably, enjoying the play on words and the aptness of the French expression as a description of the way they had seen barbecue being prepared.)

The term followed trade routes from the West Indies and quickly became known in Virginia. Before the end of the 1600s, the colony had passed a law banning the shooting of firearms at barbecues. Actually, English colonists in the lower James River settlements may have learned barbecuing from the Indi-

ans even before word spread from the Caribbean and were probably the first Europeans in the new world to adopt the practice. Since tidewater Virginia and northeastern North Carolina were similar in geography and customs, it's reasonable to assume that eastern North Carolina residents had also picked up the roasting method from native inhabitants or their northern neighbors, and they were already enjoying barbecue well before the beginning of the eighteenth century.

The Indian barbecuing method was to burn a large oak or hickory log on a grate until the coals fell through. These coals were shoveled into a hole in the ground, and the meat was placed on a rack above them to cook. With only minor variations, dressed, split pigs have been roasted over coals in just this way for over three centuries in North Carolina. The practice was so commonplace by 1728 that William Byrd of Virginia took note of it in his chronicle of the surveying of the border between his state and North Carolina. Of eastern North Carolina, Byrd wrote, "The only business here is the raising of hogs, which is managed with the least trouble and affords the diet they are most fond of. The truth of it is, the inhabitants of North Carolina devour so much swine's flesh that it fills them full of gross humors."

Since barbecue and Protestant Christianity are both cultural icons of enormous significance in North Carolina, it is only fitting that a church named after the custom came into being fairly early in the state's history. Barbecue Presbyterian Church was established in Harnett County, near Sanford, in 1757. The church actually got its name from nearby Barbecue Creek, named by a Scottish explorer, Red Neil McNeill, who said the mist rising off the stream reminded him of smoke from barbecue pits he had seen in the West Indies.

When one makes the obvious comparison between the catechisms of the various Christian denominations and the dogmas associated with different barbecue styles, it's actually somewhat surprising that there isn't an "eastern" Barbecue Church and a "western" Barbecue Church. Certainly, there is no more agreement on the fine points of doctrine between adherents of the two barbecue types than, say, a Hard Shell Baptist and a Presbyterian. But all God's children *are* unified, not only by the central tenets of the faith, but also by the overarching reality that much of the Lord's work in the state is performed with funds raised from barbecue. In fact, church barbecues have become a class unto themselves and have, as the commerce department might say, assumed a vital role in the preparation, distribution, and consumption of barbecue in North Carolina. The two biggest barbecue gatherings in North Carolina are hosted by churches, both of them, coincidentally, in Charlotte. Mallard Creek Presby-

terian Church's barbecue has been an annual event since 1929, while Williams Memorial Presbyterian started its yearly fund raiser in 1945. (Since both events are held in the fall, patrons must pass through a gauntlet of glad-handing politicians campaigning for office in order to reach the serving lines.)

Barbecue may have played a more direct role in the establishment of at least one other North Carolina church. In 1775, Henry Evans, a free black Methodist cobbler and preacher, stopped in Fayetteville on the way from Virginia to Charleston. Disturbed by the spiritual condition in which he found the African-Americans of the area, Evans decided to stay and preach, and he was soon attracting such large crowds that authorities banned him from the city. So Evans began holding clandestine meetings in the woods and sandhills, often moving from place to place to avoid harassment. (The "underground" or "invisible" church was already a southern tradition among slaves prohibited from attending regular worship services. The feeding of those who slipped away to listen to the hours of preaching at these churches was often accomplished through the barbecuing of one or two young shoats over flameless beds of coals to prevent detection.) The white Christians of Fayetteville eventually became so impressed by Evans's zeal and the obvious change in his followers that they invited him to preach openly in the city once more. Local tradition maintains that this change of heart occurred just after white citizens searching the sandhills discovered—and ate—a hastily abandoned pig barbecued at the site of one of Evans's meetings. Whether barbecue was the turning point of this drama or not, a church was built for Evans in Fayetteville, and later, a retirement home. He died in 1810, having brought Methodism to Cumberland County, the first Methodist church to Fayetteville, and probably the best barbecued pig eaten in the region up to that point.

In Ayden, near Greenville, Pete Jones's great-great-grandfather, Skilton M. Dennis, is said to have begun barbecuing pigs as early as 1830 to feed large, church camp meetings, as well as selling barbecue to the public from a chuck wagon—this was back when Ayden was known as "Ottertown" or "A Den" (as in "den of thieves"). Jones says that proves his claim that his family has been in the barbecue business longer than any other in North Carolina. But there is no record of continuous operation of a commercial barbecue business since that time. Throughout the nineteenth century, barbecuing pigs was an art largely practiced either by those entertaining friends and family or by itinerant barbecue men who plied their trade part-time at school commencements, camp meetings, fairs, and festivals.

Around 1915, Adam Scott, a black janitor and elevator operator from Goldsboro, cooked his first barbecue for a social gathering of white businessmen. The guests declared it "the best 'cue they have ever eaten," and the idea that there might be a future in barbecue was planted in Scott's mind. Although Scott continued to cater occasional parties, it wasn't until almost ten years later, when he was an employee of a local bank, that he started regularly cooking pigs on weekends in a backyard pit and selling the meat. Soon Scott was serving meals on his back porch, and by 1933, he had enclosed the porch and turned it into a dining room—one that would eventually be enlarged three times. Prominent white citizens were soon rubbing elbows with Scott's neighbors and farmers from the countryside, and patrons often had to stand in line in Scott's backyard as they waited to get into his flourishing establishment. One of those who dined on Scott's back porch, presumably without having to stand in line for too long, was the late Governor J. Melville Broughton.

Adam Scott ran the business until the late 1940s, when he turned the restaurant over to his son, Martel, Sr., and moved to Winston-Salem to become the personal barbecue chef for R.J. Reynolds, Jr. (He also had an active second career as a preacher and revivalist.) Scott's is thriving today, run by Adam's grandson, Martel, Jr., and the family name has become a household word because of Scott's commercially bottled barbecue sauce, which is sold in grocery stores across the state.

The state's first sit-down barbecue restaurant, however, was opened by Bob Melton of Rocky Mount, who died in 1958 at the age of eighty-eight after having been crowned by *Life* magazine "the king of southern barbecue." Melton was a merchant and horse trader who started cooking barbecue around Rocky Mount as a hobby in 1919. He built a barbecue shed on the Tar River in 1922, and two years later, he built a restaurant on the same quiet, shady spot where a rebuilt Melton's stands today. (It was also a flood-

prone spot, and patrons occasionally had to row to Melton's in boats to pick up an order of barbecue.) Melton is also widely considered to be the man who firmly established the style of preparing barbecue that much of eastern North Carolina later adopted as its own: whole hogs cooked over oak or hickory coals, finely chopped and fairly dry, and seasoned before serving with a touch of the same sauce used to baste the roasting pig—vinegar, salt, black pepper, and red pepper (finely ground *and* in flakes). Rocky Mount, a railroad and tobacco-market town, was a barbecue

Adam Scott

Bob Melton

Bob Melton's original restaurant, built adjacent to the flood-prone Tar River.

center for years before neighboring Wilson weighed in with several restaurants. Goldsboro, thanks to Adam Scott, had long been touting its own barbecue tradition. Even today, those three cities—Rocky Mount, Wilson, and Goldsboro—account for the vast majority of good barbecue restaurants in eastern North Carolina by almost anyone's reckoning.

A good distance to the west, in the town of Lexington, quite a different barbecue heritage was being established during the early 1900s. A few barbecuers who had become adept at using hardwood to roast pork *shoulders*—

as opposed to the whole pig—for special occasions started holding occasional public cook-outs, dubbing the events "Everybody's Day." Soon some of these barbecuers began cooking for an entire week at a time when court was being held, since the court session brought a steady stream of country dwellers to town. In 1919, Sid Weaver and George Ridenhour put up a tent opposite the court-house that became the first more or less permanent barbecue stand in Lexington. Not long afterwards, Jess Swicegood put up a tent directly alongside that one and went into head-to-head competition with Weaver, who

NORTH CAROLINA BARBECUE : *Flavored by Time*

Lexington barbecue pioneer Sid Weaver (left)

Courtesy Keith and Charles Stamey

had already bought out Ridenhour. Weaver later replaced his tent with a small building, and Swicegood followed suit.

It was at this point that one of North Carolina's most impressive barbecue legacies began to develop. Around 1927, C. Warner Stamey, a high school student, began working part-time for Jess Swicegood, learning the art of slow cooking pork shoulders over oak and hickory coals for nine to ten hours, then removing the skin and fat and gently pulling the meat apart into chunks—the larger ones for slicing, the smaller for chopping. The meat was roasted with no basting, but was moistened before serving with ingredients matching the basic eastern sauce, to which a small amount of catsup and sugar had been added.

Stamey dreamed early on of having his own place, and in 1930, he moved to Shelby and opened a barbecue restaurant modeled after Swicegood's first stand, a tent with sawdust on the floor. During the next few years, he

Lexington's Jess Swicegood at his original barbecue stand
Courtesy Lexington Barbecue Festival

NORTH CAROLINA BARBECUE : *Flavored by Time*

Warner Stamey (right) taught Lexington methods to many other successful barbecuers.

Courtesy Lexington Barbecue Festival

taught the Lexington method to his wife's brother, Alston Bridges, and to Red Bridges (no relation). When Stamey moved back to Lexington in the mid-1930s, he left behind two men whose Lexington-style barbecue fiefdoms would flourish in Shelby for the next sixty years, with reputations extending across the South. Alston Bridges Barbecue and (Red) Bridges Barbecue Lodge are still family-run operations, and they still serve barbecue cooked with the secrets patiently passed along by Warner Stamey.

In 1938, Stamey bought the place in Lexington where he had first learned his trade from Jess Swicegood. In the early '50s, at that same location, he taught the business and his special methods to a young man named Wayne Monk. Monk is the longtime owner and operator of Lexington Barbecue (which used to be called Lexington Barbecue #1), and today, he is probably the most accomplished and famous barbecue guru in North Carolina.

But the Stamey influence had not finished

A Three-Hundred-Year Tradition

spreading. Stamey moved to Greensboro and opened a restaurant at a site on High Point Road; it's now a landmark, sitting opposite the Greensboro Coliseum. The new Greensboro restaurant opened in 1953, and about that time, Stamey—a tireless innovator when it came to pit design, menu modification, and countless other refinements—tried another experiment that changed the North Carolina barbecue experience forever. Before the '50s, barbecue had been routinely served on or with white bread or rolls (except for the occasional baked corn bread in the east). Borrowing a feature from the fish camps he had visited, Stamey began serving hush puppies—balls or fingers of deep-fried corn-meal batter—with his barbecue. Today, with very few exceptions, hush puppies are considered the standard accompaniment to barbecue and are served from one end of North Carolina to the other. (Pete Jones's Skylight Inn and B's Barbecue serve squares of baked corn bread, while several eastern North Carolina establishments offer corn sticks—long, slender pieces of corn bread that are baked, then deep fried.)

To this day, rolls are optional with barbecue at Stamey's two Greensboro restaurants and are routinely eaten instead of hush puppies by Stamey's son, Keith, who now runs the family operation with his brother Charles. The original Stamey's drive-in on High Point Road has been replaced by a beautiful ranch-style restaurant, and just inside the front door hangs a portrait of Warner Stamey, the man who spread the gospel of Lexington-style barbecue far and wide.

While some legendary, older barbecue restaurants are being run by second- and third-generation family members, other well-known places have gone out of business in recent years, in some cases because the owner's families weren't interested in carrying on the tradition. Very few new barbecue spots have opened recently, and many of those among the newer generations of restaurant operators say they aren't willing to invest the long hours and backbreaking work necessary to produce great barbecue. On the other hand, interest in barbecue has probably never been higher among consumers, and these fires are fanned by specialized barbecue newsletters and by dozens of pig cooking contests and festivals spread across North Carolina, from Wilmington to Tryon. In 1977, columnist Jerry Bledsoe wrote a piece urging the city of Lexington to "bring back 'Everybody's Day,' throw up the tents and have a big annual barbecue festival with music and dancing and other festivities to celebrate this regional delicacy." A few years later, Lexington began doing exactly that, and today, the Lexington Barbecue Festival is the largest such event in the state. In 1995, the festival attracted over 150,000 people, with some twelve thousand pounds of barbecue served. Considering the

NORTH CAROLINA BARBECUE : *Flavored by Time*

current popularity of what must be considered a dwindling art, we have to face the probability that North Carolina will have fewer really great barbecue places in the years ahead, but those that remain should thrive for a long time to come.

Stamey's original Greensboro restaurant opened in 1953.

Courtesy Keith and Charles Stamey

Mitchell's serves pit-cooked barbecue and home-style vegetables, prepared and served by Doretha, Ed, Steven, and Aubrey (not pictured).

A North Carolina Barbecue Primer

The World's Best Barbecue?

◼◻◼◻◼◻◼Here's an issue that will be eternally subjective, drawing personal taste, regional chauvinism, hyperbole, and friendly boasting into a cacophony of competing claims that will never be settled in our lifetime.

There's no question that there *are* pundits who have pronounced North Carolina barbecue the best they've ever eaten. Craig Claiborne, food columnist for the *New York Times*, has eaten in most of the country's best-known barbecue joints over the years, and has stated unequivocally that the chopped pork served in North Carolina—both east and west—is definitely his favorite. *National Geographic* picked Pete Jones's Skylight Inn in Ayden as its world-champion barbecue spot a few years back. And *Southern* magazine recognized Wilber's in Goldsboro as home of "The South's Best Barbecue." (This is even higher praise than it seems at first glance. How much really great barbecue can there be outside the South anyway?)

Other material can be brought in to support the claim. In the early 1980s, several developments helped gild the state's barbecue reputation, beginning with a well-publicized debate between congressmen Gene Johnston of North Carolina and John Napier of South Carolina as to which state produces the best barbecue. To settle the issue, several restaurants from the two states each ended up sending twenty to thirty pounds of barbecue to a big contest and barbecue banquet held in Washington. The 1981 event ended in a draw, but in 1982, Short Sugar's of Reidsville was declared the winner of the so-called North-South Carolina Barbecue Bowl. The following year, North Carolina's claim to barbecue superiority was further enhanced when President Reagan, eager to show off the best in authentic American cuisine, invited Wayne Monk of Lexington Barbecue to feed several European heads of state at a major international economic summit held in Williamsburg, Virginia. And in 1984, Hursey's of Burlington was named champion in the North-South Carolina Barbecue Bowl.

Native North Carolinians can naturally be expected to assert that the very best barbecue comes from right here in the Tar Heel State—especially if they end up moving to another state. In the late 1970s, North Carolina native Barry Farber—a controversial New York City radio talk-show host and unsuccessful mayoral candidate in the Big Apple— arranged with a Times Square restaurant to serve North Carolina barbecue prepared and shipped by Fuzzy's in Madison. (The ven-

ture eventually failed, reportedly because the barbecue wasn't properly presented to the New Yorkers.) Former UNC cheerleader Zacki Murphy of Hillsborough, a veteran model and television spokesperson, has likewise been preoccupied for years with the challenge of introducing North Carolina barbecue to New Yorkers. Zacki started out selling PBQ—her term for pit-cooked barbecue— from a vending cart on the streets of New York in between modeling and TV assignments; later she moved to a small storefront restaurant. Zacki's barbecue, like Farber's, was pit cooked by Fuzzy's in Madison, but then it was mixed with her own special Lexington-style sauce and fast frozen for quick delivery via truck. Although neither of these initial ventures lasted, Murphy has vowed to persist with the barbecue business, either in New York or, perhaps, back home in North Carolina. Meanwhile, New York designer Alexander Julian, a native of Chapel Hill, is fond of quipping that he designed the basketball uniforms for the NBA's Charlotte Hornets at least partly in exchange for regular shipments of North Carolina barbecue, which he says is unmatched anywhere in the world.

There's something else to this sort of playful barbecue boasting, and it has to do with the need to define who we are as individuals in a mass culture. Alan Pridgen, formerly an English professor at Chowan College in northeastern North Carolina, explored this idea in a scholarly paper he once presented to an academic conference on popular culture. He suggested that the urge to seek out and consume the *best* barbecue may be a subconscious search for an identity "rooted in a past of Jeffersonian small farmers who lived out their lives in close-knit families and communities where self-sufficiency, independence and social intimacy and trust were prized." According to Pridgen, "These values are symbolically imbedded in the contemporary North Carolinian's passion for his unique food and his unique culture"—all the more so, he says, since that culture has sometimes been characterized as impoverished and unsophisticated by mainstream America.

But if rating barbecue is all tied up in traditional values and pride of place—as well as a sort of reverse snobbery—the experiences of growing up invariably carry the most weight, meaning the best barbecue will probably be found in or near one's own hometown. On the other hand, those city dwellers or suburbanites who discover barbecue later in life have the pleasure of choosing from among various ready-made, secondhand rural identities, and settling on a favorite style of barbecue can be as much fun as dressing up in boots and a cowboy hat or developing a southern drawl.

The best? It obviously depends on who you talk to. But one thing that *is* certain is that North Carolina barbecue is different from what you'll find everywhere else. I believe it's the only kind of barbecue in which the meat itself is the centerpiece rather than the smoke, the pepper, or the sauce. North Carolina pork, barbecued to perfection, has a naturally rich, sweet taste that is delicately flavored by smoke—not overcome by it like something dragged from a burning house. The slow-roasted, chopped meat should have an overall light pink to light brown shade, appealingly set off by flecks of dark brown outside meat, and it should not be reddened by a smoke ring. Whether it's sliced or chopped, North Carolina 'cue at its best is moist (even before sauce), yet not laced with fat—meltingly tender, yet firm in consistency, with the meat shredded into coarse fibers. And it should never be mushy or appear to be held together by congealed fat. Whether the preferred sauce is the peppery eastern variety or the milder, sweeter Lexington style, it is meant to merely add accent to the meat, not to cling like wallpaper paste or smother it with the taste of liquid hickory smoke, catsup, molasses, sugar, bell pepper, or chili powder.

Let me point out here that I like the best examples of many types of barbecue from around the country: Memphis-style pulled pig, ribs (basted in sauce or treated with a dry-spice rub), Texas-style beef brisket, chicken, sausage—whatever. But the aroma of pork roasting over hardwood coals draws

A North Carolina Barbecue Primer

me like a siren song, along with the thought of treating my tongue to a warm, yielding barbecue sandwich on a cloud-soft bun, the sweet, tender shreds of pork perfectly complemented by a fiery hint of pepper and vinegar and the piquancy of coleslaw. Unless it's really important to you, I suggest you leave off worrying about which is best—and simply enjoy North Carolina barbecue for what it is, and because it's unlike any other.

The Great Divide: East Versus West

It could well be that the feuding between the eastern, or coastal plain, and piedmont portions of the state has cost North Carolina a preeminent position in the nation's barbecue consciousness. Let's face it—we make it tough for someone outside the state to conclude that North Carolina serves the country's best barbecue when we can't even decide among ourselves what good barbecue is. I mean . . . are we that unsure about it? People from other states may be dead wrong in claiming that their barbecue is better than ours, but at least they will usually pull together and argue for *their* native version with a passion and zeal that, in our case, falls exhausted in the dust somewhere between Lexington and Goldsboro.

On the other hand, we North Carolinians can certainly argue that we get more fun out of our barbecue than anyone else in America, not only in the eating experience, but also by keeping our barbecue arguments inside the state where we can enjoy them to the fullest—and to heck with what outsiders think. "You think they cook better pig in Memphis? Fine. . . that leaves more of the real stuff for the rest of us."

But if you're going to get the most mileage out of the debate, you need to be up on the real differences between the styles of barbecue served up in the east and in the piedmont. Actually the two types are more commonly known as "eastern" and either "Lexington" or "western," although the latter is something of a misnomer since western North Carolina—the mountain area—is practically another state when it comes to barbecue. (You may find something *called* barbecue in some of the tourist destinations in the Smokies, but like the typical feathered, plains-Indian headdress worn and sold in Cherokee, it isn't authentic to this state, but is an import from the West.) For our purposes, "western" refers to the North Carolina piedmont—from somewhere between Tryon on the west to Raleigh on the east.

You should also be aware that some quite knowledgeable barbecue enthusiasts think there isn't much difference between the two styles. The *New York Times*'s Craig Claiborne wrote, "To an experienced North Carolina barbecue addict, the difference between the Lexington and Down East versions might be pronounced. To me, they were subtle, the main one being the sauce ingredients. And even the absence of a slight tomato tang in the Down East sauce didn't make a whole lot of difference—vinegar is the key factor in both of them."

Much ado about nothing—or is there a significant difference between east and west? No matter what you decide, you'll have a wonderful time doing the research.

Eastern-Style Barbecue

Eastern North Carolina barbecue is *the* original American barbecue. (Even though barbecue probably originated in seventeenth-century Virginia, eastern-style barbecue generally hasn't survived well in the Old Dominion and is difficult to find there.) This coastal-plain barbecue is nearly always prepared from whole hogs. In earlier days, the split pigs were roasted over pits dug in the ground, into which oak or hickory coals were shoveled from a separate fire. Later, the pits moved under shelters or into sheds separated from the main restaurant and became vertical structures: rectangular boxes of brick or cinder block from two to three feet high, with the grill resting a little below a top that is covered by a lid that can be raised and lowered. The coals are spread at the bottom, around two feet below the grill, where they are fanned by air circulating through vents near the floor. Some eastern pits used to have a metal layer several inches *above* the grill on which coals were spread, so that heat came from both top and bottom, eliminating the need to turn the pig midway through the cooking process. (Nowadays, so many eastern North Carolina barbecue houses have begun cooking with gas or electricity that commercially designed cookers predominate in this region.) The usual practice in the east is to begin roasting the hogs skin-side-up for the first few hours, then turn them meat-side-up. During the cooking process, the meat is periodically basted with the same sauce used later to season the chopped barbecue.

True eastern North Carolina barbecue sauce is different from that you'll find anywhere else in the United States in that it contains no tomato extracts. It seems seventeenth- and eighteenth-century colonists wouldn't have considered eating tomatoes because of the prevailing belief that they were poisonous, and they often seasoned their pit-roasted pig with vinegar seasoned with peppers and oysters. This is still the basic sauce used in the east both for basting the pigs as they cook and seasoning the barbecue once it's chopped— it consists primarily of vinegar, water, salt, black pepper, red pepper, and both finely ground cayenne and the dried, crushed

Pit cooking whole pigs near Rocky Mount, 1944

Courtesy N.C. Division of Archives and History

variety (but no oysters). It is a fiery blend, the chief sensory impression being of hot, salty vinegar. There are literally thousands of variations on the basic recipe, and someone's favorite sauce is likely to include a dozen other spices—their identities a closely guarded secret—but every sauce will at least begin with the vinegar-salt-pepper trinity. A true eastern sauce not only has no tomatoes: it also has no added sugar, molasses, corn syrup, or other sweeteners—although some eastern barbecuers will occasionally add some form of sweetener to a "dipping" sauce to be served at a pig picking, leaving it out of sauce to be used for basting and seasoning the chopped barbecue.

Sometimes eastern North Carolina barbecue is seasoned "dry" after it's chopped, meaning salt, black pepper, and red pepper are sprinkled on and mixed into the chopped meat, which is then moistened with plain vinegar. Barbecue seasoned in this way is likely to find its way to your plate speckled with visible crushed red-pepper flakes or seeds.

The importance of sauce or seasonings to the overall taste of eastern North Carolina barbecue has grown in recent years, as more and more of the big-name barbecuers have begun roasting their pigs with gas or electricity rather than cooking over hardwood coals. (More on this subject later in this chapter.)

Despite the prevalence of basting in the coastal plain, much eastern barbecue also seems to have a drier consistency than that found in the piedmont. This is partially because of the drier "white" meat from hams and tenderloin that goes into whole-hog barbecue. It may also have something to do with the fact that many high-volume eastern barbecue houses have stopped chopping their cooked pork by hand, opting instead to use a machine. This machine not only gives a finer, "minced" texture to the barbecue but also tends to dry it out a bit. The writer James Vilas, who wrote an article for *Esquire* years ago called "My Pig Beats Your Cow" described the eastern product as "dry, salty barbecue."

But the more arid barbecue of the east is superbly complemented by the side dish that most often accompanies it: Brunswick stew—whose sweetness contrasts perfectly with the saltiness of the meat, and whose extravagant moistness balances eastern barbecue's drier texture. Some folks—myself included—enjoy mixing a dollop or two of this thick, reddish orange stew into a serving of eastern barbecue. Brunswick stew was originally made with squirrel meat, but today it most often contains chicken and/or pork and/or beef. In my opinion, Brunswick stew that is to be served with barbecue should contain only boned chicken, tomatoes, potatoes, onions, corn, and lima beans, plus seasonings. Shredded,

A North Carolina Barbecue Primer

cooked pork can be added if the stew is not to be served as an accompaniment to pork, but I still prefer only white meat—no beef—in this dish. If cream-style corn is used, as it often is in the east, little further sweetening is necessary; otherwise, sugar is generally added with a heavier hand. Brunswick stew is less likely to accompany barbecue in the piedmont, becoming increasingly rare as you move westward, and when you do find it, it's often a "throw-everything-you-can-reach-into-the-pot" mishmash.

Almost as traditional as Brunswick stew as an eastern side dish are the ubiquitous "barbecued" potatoes found throughout the coastal plain. These have a bland or ever-so-slightly sweet taste that perfectly offsets the acidity of the tart, peppery barbecue. They're really nothing more than white potatoes cut in large chunks and boiled, often with a little onion, tomato sauce, sugar, and bacon drippings added to the water in the pot. But while boiled potatoes are an eastern staple, they pretty much disappear in barbecue spots west of the Raleigh city limits.

Hush puppies are nearly universal in all North Carolina barbecue restaurants, but corn sticks are another firmly entrenched eastern barbecue tradition, particularly around Raleigh and Wilson. These are slender, eight-inch fingers of corn bread that are first baked in a mold, then fried in a deep-fat cooker. The outside of a corn stick has a crunchy texture similar to that of a hush puppy, but the inside is heavier and more dense, and has a taste similar to corn bread baked without baking powder or flour. As a matter of fact, some eastern barbecue houses, such as Pete Jones's Skylight Inn in Ayden and B's in Greenville, serve plain, baked corn bread—simply cornmeal, salt, eggs, and water—rather than either corn sticks or hush puppies. (One idiosyncrasy of eastern North Carolinians is that they often use the universal term "corn bread" to refer to all corn-meal-based concoctions, whether baked, griddled, or deep fried.)

Because Brunswick stew, barbecued potatoes, and even fried chicken are served so often as side dishes in eastern barbecue houses, coleslaw is more of a garnish in the east than it is in the piedmont, where slaw and hush puppies are likely to be the only accompaniment to the barbecue itself. The slaw of the east will ordinarily contain either mayonnaise or a mayonnaise-mustard mixture, so that it ranges in color from white to bright yellow. Sweet pickle cubes are often included in the eastern version, along with celery seed. Once in a while, you'll run across eastern slaw that's simply moistened with vinegar and sugar, with no mayonnaise or mustard.

In eastern North Carolina, barbecue has a strong and pleasant association with the region's tobacco culture. In the days before modern bulk curing, when tobacco was still hand picked, hand tied onto sticks, and hung in the rafters of the curing barn by hand, many farmers would celebrate the completion of this exhausting process by holding a festive barbecue for the dozens of "hands" who had worked to put in the crop. A pig would be barbecued over an open pit, often dug beneath the shelter of the tobacco barn, and the meat would be chopped, then served out of a large wooden tub. Today, the conclusion of the harvest is still often marked by barbecues and pig pickings. It is no coincidence that the best eastern barbecue restaurants are in the tobacco-market towns of Rocky Mount, Wilson, and Goldsboro. It is at these restaurants where farmers often celebrate selling their tobacco with a convivial barbecue meal with friends and associates. In this region, more than anywhere else, barbecue is the food that bespeaks good times and is a treat to be savored in the company of others.

Lexington (Western)-Style Barbecue

In the North Carolina piedmont, barbecue is nearly universally derived from pork shoulders, rather than from the entire pig. No one seems to know how the preference for pork shoulders began in this region, but photographs clearly show that this regional peculiarity was already established by the late 1920s. Modern-day experts like Wayne Monk of Lexington Barbecue say shoulders are easier to handle, and they produce not only juicier barbecue, but also far less waste than whole pigs. Still, you can't help wondering why the whole-pig tradition dominates the restaurants of the east, then disappears so abruptly at the geographic fall line that delineates the edge of the coastal plain and the beginning of the piedmont. Western-style shoulders are usually slow cooked for nine to twelve hours, and covered with foil or cardboard to keep the ashes off. They're cooked meat-side-down for the first four hours or so, then turned. In this part of the state, meat is seldom basted as it cooks, probably because the relatively high fat content of the pork shoulders makes it unnecessary.

The Lexington-style shoulders are often cooked in chimneyed pits that form one wall of the restaurant kitchen. Two rows of metal doors typically provide access, the lower for spreading coals and the upper for adding, turning, or removing the meat. (Some piedmont restaurants, particularly around Stanley and Rowan Counties, northwest of Charlotte, cook on waist-high pits that simply vent into the open air when their covers are raised—like the ones common in the east. Because of the smoke, these are usually located in buildings separate from the kitchen.) Regardless of which type of pit is used, the cooking

H. Lee Waters

Barbecuing pork shoulders for Lexington political rally, early 1930s

North Carolina Collection

University of North Carolina Library at Chapel Hill

NORTH CAROLINA BARBECUE : *Flavored by Time*

shed or kitchen will have some type of central firebox, often with an opening both to the outside, where wood can be added to the fire, and to the inside, where coals are removed by shovel and sprinkled beneath the cooking shoulders in the individual pits.

There are significant differences between east and west in the way barbecued pork is served. Western or Lexington-style barbecue is traditionally available either chopped, "coarse-chopped" into chunks, or even sliced, whereas eastern barbecue is almost always rather finely chopped. Hand-chopped barbecue in the piedmont is usually chunkier than the eastern version, except for the machine-shredded variety, which is identical to its eastern counterpart in consistency. It's also interesting to note that in most Lexington-style barbecue houses throughout the piedmont, you can special order "outside brown" meat, either chopped or sliced. This is the slightly crusty, chewy, well-browned meat (*not* skin) from the portion of the shoulder where the fat and skin have been stripped away to expose the lean meat before cooking. Many customers in the piedmont will order no other portion, and personally, "outside brown" is my absolute favorite part of any piece of barbecued pork.

In general, barbecue in the piedmont seems more moist than the eastern variety, despite its lean appearance on the plate. First of all, shoulders have darker meat and are more marbled with fat than most other parts of the pig—an average fifteen-pound shoulder will slowly drip seven or eight pounds of fat down through the inside of the meat and onto the coals during the nine to ten hours the shoulders are on the pit. But this natural basting isn't the only factor. Since the barbecue is usually not chopped as fine as it is in the east, the meat seems to retain more of its moisture. Then too, Lexington-style barbecuers usually serve their meat with more of the sauce ladled over it than do their eastern cousins. Some piedmont establishments offer "minced" barbecue: meat that's nearly pulverized, then mixed with copious amounts of sauce to form a sort of "sloppy-joe" mixture. (As you can see, this is not one of my personal favorites.)

No other variance between the two distinct barbecue regions of the state is as vociferously discussed and debated as the difference between eastern and Lexington sauce, although I personally believe that it's a distinction in search of a difference. Basically, you take a typical eastern-style vinegar-salt-pepper sauce, you add just enough catsup and maybe a little Worcestershire to darken the sauce to a deep reddish brown, then you throw in a little brown sugar—just enough to cut the bite of the vinegar a bit. That's it. That's the big difference all the shouting and arguing is about. Oh, there may be a few other spices in there, but the basic taste is

A North Carolina Barbecue Primer

Eastern-style barbecue is typically served with coleslaw, boiled potatoes, Brunswick stew, and hush puppies.

Lexington-style barbecue, served chopped and sliced

NORTH CAROLINA BARBECUE : *Flavored by Time*

still vinegar and pepper. For some reason, a lot of people in the east seem to have the mistaken notion that western or Lexington-style sauce is usually thick with catsup and molasses, like the barbecue sauces found in Texas or on your supermarket shelf. But while those who developed piedmont barbecue obviously were no longer afraid to eat tomatoes, they didn't go hog-wild with them either. Yes, Lexington-style sauce does contain some tomato extracts, but it's usually a relatively thin sauce, not that much different in color or consistency from the traditional eastern sauce, which is itself usually red from all the ground red pepper that's added. The taste of the sugar, frankly, is hardly noticeable to most people since it's overridden by the heat of the black and red peppers. Actually, the biggest difference is the name: most piedmont barbecue places refer to their particular formulation as "dip," rather than sauce. Piedmont restaurants typically season their barbecue with their regular sauce in the kitchen, then offer a hotter, less-sweet version on the table.

I should mention that not all piedmont barbecuers think of their product as "Lexington" style. The sauce served over the traditional chopped shoulders in several Rowan and Stanly County establishments definitely has more of a vinegar-and-hot-pepper base, with less tomato taste than traditional Lexington dip. And the coleslaw at these places is noticeably more tart. Considering these differences, it's no great surprise to find that there's been a running disagreement between Lexington and Salisbury, in Rowan County, as to which community was the first to introduce barbecue in a big way. According to local records, John Blackwelder of Salisbury added a barbecue pit to his taxi stand in 1918, one year before Sid Weaver put up his barbecue tent near the Lexington courthouse. The popularity of Blackwelder's barbecue—originally prepared from pork loins rather than shoulders—is said to have quickly spread far and wide due to word-of-mouth reports from the railway workers who became customers as they traveled up and down the line. But of course, the same railway line runs through Lexington, and there is little doubt that the reputation of Lexington's barbecue, if not its quality, soon eclipsed Salisbury's.

The difference between eastern and piedmont barbecue extends to the side dishes as well. If you were led blindfolded into a barbecue restaurant, then had the blindfold removed at the table, you could easily tell ninety percent of the time whether you were in the east or the piedmont by one glance at the coleslaw served with your barbecue. Western slaw is almost always red, and it has a totally different taste and texture than its eastern cousin. Whereas eastern slaw ranges in texture from shredded to nearly pulverized, Lexington-style slaw is almost always chopped into crunchy bits about the size of BBs. It's

A North Carolina Barbecue Primer

basically seasoned with barbecue sauce instead of either mustard or mayonnaise, so it's pepper-hot and vinegar-tangy, and it's also fairly sweet, since more sugar is added than normally goes into the barbecue dip. Some fence-straddling places in Durham, Orange, and Alamance—counties near the dividing line between the piedmont and the coastal plain—serve western-style barbecue but eastern-style slaw, which seems to be clear evidence of a sort of barbecue split personality. East meets west head-on at the A&M Grill in Mebane, which serves pit-cooked shoulders with—Lord help us—*pink* coleslaw, dressed with a mixture of mayonnaise and barbecue sauce.

Hush puppies are served nearly universally with barbecue in the west, just as they are in the east. As I've mentioned elsewhere, the descendants of Warner Stamey claim that he was the first—at least in the piedmont—to borrow the idea from fish camps, figuring the traditional accompaniment to fried catfish would also go well with barbecue. The hush puppies in the piedmont seem to me to be generally skinnier than the ones in the east, but this is probably because most places in either region buy their mechanical hush puppy–forming machines from the same supplier. Smaller places usually still hand-squeeze their hush puppy batter through a pastry tube into the frying oil, or drop it into the deep fryer by knife, spoon, or scoop. Old menus and photos do indicate that rolls or even plain, white loaf bread were generally served with barbecue in the '20s and '30s, and they're both available at some places even today, east *and* west.

While there may be sandwiches, hot dogs, and other non-barbecue items on the menu, don't look for Brunswick stew, barbecued potatoes, fried chicken, or vegetables served as accompaniments to barbecue in the west. A barbecue *tray* will contain only barbecue, coleslaw, and hush puppies, whereas a barbecue *plate* will have all of the above plus french fries. There are some notable dessert offerings in the piedmont, including banana pudding topped with meringue at Fuzzy's (Madison), peach cobbler and ice cream at Stamey's (Greensboro), fried pies at Mitchell's (Wilson), and a variety of outstanding homemade desserts at Allen & Son (Chapel Hill).

The biggest difference betwen the two styles is that there are still a lot more places in the piedmont than in the east where the barbecue delivers a genuine wood-cooked taste. While there has been a disturbing piedmont trend toward the use of electric cookers in recent years, the expectations about whether barbecue is *supposed* to taste of wood smoke is still the great divide that will probably differentiate east and west forever.

Old Fashioned Pit Cooking: Does It Really Matter?

There is simply no escaping the fact that thousands and thousands of people across North Carolina smack their lips every day over so-called barbecue that's never been anywhere near a wood-burning pit. North Carolina Department of Agriculture regulations state that pork cooked over gas flames or in an electric cooker cannot be labeled "barbecue" if it's packaged for sale in stores; instead it must be labeled "cooked pork." However, there are no such regulations covering what's served in restaurants, and an incredible number of barbecue places—including most of the best-known spots in the east, and a growing number in the west—have converted from hardwood to gas or electricity.

This transformation goes directly to the heart of the matter, to the very definition of "barbecue." After all, can and should it properly be called "barbecue" if it isn't cooked over wood coals? Well, while a couple of *Webster*'s definitions for barbecue describe meat broiled or roasted over an open fire, another says the *verb* barbecue means "to broil or cook meat with a highly seasoned sauce." The old hands will vigorously denounce such a definition, but there it is—and you can hardly deny that, like it or not, it pretty well describes the way things are in a lot of areas

in our state: sauce has replaced pit cooking as the defining factor, the key ingredient in barbecue.

There's been a lot of talk about health department rules being responsible for the change, but the fact is that I haven't found a single case in which a county health department ever made an existing, wood-cooking barbecue place convert to gas or electricity. Even if, in some counties, new restaurants aren't allowed to build and operate a wood-burning pit, existing businesses are almost always covered by so-called "grandfather" clauses, meaning that they can continue to cook with wood if they so choose.

The plain fact is that a lot of places that built their reputations on real, honest-to-goodness pit-cooked barbecue fall victim to their own success. With a few notable exceptions, real pit cooking is mostly considered feasible for restaurants doing a small-to-moderate volume, and owners become convinced that it will be difficult to expand their business and maximize profits without changing. They feel compelled to switch to a cooking method that will not only allow them to handle ever-increasing volume, but also solve some of the labor problems associated with wood cooking. Nearly all the real open-pit barbecue houses have someone who's been with the business for twenty or thirty years; who's willing to stay up all night or come to work in the wee hours to tend the pits; who performs a hot, dirty, back-breaking job few others are willing to do—and who will be very difficult to replace once they retire. And in addition to all that, hardwood is becoming more expensive and harder to find, especially hickory wood. Pete Jones of the moderately sized Skylight Inn in Ayden says he burns between 125 and 200 cords of oak yearly to cook his barbecue, while a larger establishment like Wilber's in Goldsboro—probably the largest open-pit barbecue place in North Carolina—no doubt uses twice that amount.

While the temptations to change to gas or electricity are understandable, why is it that all but a handful of places in the east have made the switch, while a majority of barbecue places in the piedmont have stuck with the messier, more expensive hardwood pits? My own theory is that eastern North Carolinians, with their large-scale farming mentality, tend to be immensely practical people, always ready to find a quicker, more efficient way to do anything. (I've observed this trait firsthand among my two brothers-in-law, who both operate large farms in the northeastern part of the state.) In the piedmont, on the other hand, I believe the old ways tend to be more carefully preserved, if for no other reason than to provide a comforting and needed contrast to the high technology and frantic pace of the large cities located there.

The really strange thing to me is that,

practicality aside, so many eastern North Carolinians, having grown up with world-renowned pit-cooked barbecue, have acquiesced in this wholesale societal transformation with so little protest. The only possible answer is that Tar Heels from the coastal plain have consumed so much barbecue over the years in restaurants and at catered gatherings of every description that it has gradually become a more or less generic food to them. Somewhere along the line, the requirement that barbecue have a wood-smoked taste was lost, so that the word *barbecue* became subconsciously redefined to describe tender, tasty roast pork, well seasoned with salt, vinegar, and a mixture of hot peppers—or, to use the agriculture department's term for the grocery-store stuff in plastic containers, simply *cooked pork*. This is the only possible explanation for the continued loyalty and enthusiasm of customers at well-known eastern restaurants that have switched from open pits to gas or electricity—restaurants like Scott's in Goldsboro, or Bob Melton's in Rocky Mount. The patrons' tastes can only have evolved as their memories have faded.

Now let me hasten to say that merely cooking on an open pit is no guarantee that the end product will be acceptable—and that three of the four things necessary to produce great barbecue can be done very well on a gas or electric cooker. Of the four key factors—tenderness, consistency, wood-smoked

Pork shoulders roasting on enclosed pit

taste, and seasoning—only the real, delicate wood-smoked taste obtained from hardwood coals can't be duplicated over gas or electricity. Some restaurateurs have tried using electric smokers to give their barbecue this characteristic, but in my view, this tends to give the meat an oversmoked or artificially smoked flavor. Proponents of gas or electric cookers say the big advantage is that temperature can be controlled precisely at a low level over a long period of time, producing meat that is exceptionally tender because of the extremely slow cooking. However, the owner of Wilber's in Goldsboro—a proponent of open-pit cooking—promotes a different view. Wilber Shirley says, "With other burners, you cook the hog with the heat on top. Cooking our way, with the fire underneath, the juices drip down through the meat and onto the coals. That dripping makes the meat softer and gives it its flavor."

My own experience has been that much

of the pork cooked on gas or electric cookers *is* extremely tender and juicy without becoming limp. But at this point, with the wood-smoked taste completely absent, the barbecuer has only one remaining ingredient to work with: seasoning. Many gas or electric cooker enthusiasts will tell you in all earnestness that since the wood-smoke taste was so delicate to begin with, most people won't even notice its absence, provided the sauce is done just right. A lot of them have tinkered with their sauce ingredients or dry seasonings to the point that they believe they're creating barbecue that's every bit as tender and flavorful as the original pit-cooked version . . . and their customers are backing them up by saying things like, "The barbecue tastes just like it always has."

So what's a fellow to do: retreat to a stubbornly held position and refuse to budge—or try to keep an open mind? In a *New York Times* column, Tom Wicker said he defends the rights of those who have switched to gas or electricity, then went on to growl, "But to anyone deeply into barbecue, the idea of cooking it any way but over live coals is repugnant." Personally, I take a more forgiving attitude. I have to say that while I have tasted some very tender, well-seasoned, and extremely tasty chopped roast pork prepared on gas or electric cookers, I'm just not sure I feel comfortable calling it *barbecue*. On the other hand, I've tasted some stringy, tough, dried-out barbecue that was cooked over hardwood coals; and given a choice, I wouldn't have selected it over the tastier roast pork simply because it was pit cooked. In the last analysis, I suppose people have a right to define barbecue any way they darn well please: who am I to say they're wrong? For reasons that may well be emotional as much as taste oriented, I much prefer a wood-smoked flavor in my barbecue, but I'll concede that there are some places out there whose barbecue I'll happily consume without asking too many questions.

While the number of barbecue places in the piedmont that have given up pit cooking is growing, every barbecue restaurateur with any kind of aspiration to a regional reputation still has a sizable woodpile outside the restaurant where it's readily visible. (One or two sneaky souls have switched to electric cookers but keep their woodpiles for camouflage!)

Most barbecue restaurants use a mixture of oak and hickory, a few spots use only hickory, while a few others swear by hardwood charcoal. Some foresters maintain that once hardwood is reduced to coals, it makes no difference what kind it is in terms of the flavor it produces in food. That argument seems to be disproved by the current popularity of mesquite, which definitely lends a very distinctive flavor to many grilled foods, although—thankfully—North Carolina barbecue is not among them. (Mesquite is actually more of a large shrub than a genuine hardwood.) My own perception is that hickory imparts a flavor that is at least recognizable, if not superior to that of oak, although oak is probably the wood most commonly used for cooking barbecue in the piedmont. But having said that, I'm not positive I could consistently pass a blind taste test to discern the difference between barbecue cooked over hickory, oak, or even hardwood charcoal, and to my way of thinking, slow cooking over any of these three types of coals will produce outstanding results.

Unfortunately, it seems certain that the number of barbecue restaurateurs willing to stick with the inconvenience and extra work of pit cooking is bound to diminish in the years ahead. Jimmy Harvey of Jimmy's Barbecue in Lexington predicts that nearly everyone will go to gas or electricity in five to ten years because cooking with wood is so much work, and Wayne Monk of Lexington Barbecue has warned that his restaurant, too, may have to take that step one day. Keith Allen of Chapel Hill's Allen & Son—who works as hard as anyone in the state to turn out great, hickory-cooked barbecue—put it this way: "The younger generation doesn't want to work that hard; they're more interested in computers and profits. The old way will disappear when the old hearts go out with it."

Barbecue Outside North Carolina

If you live in North Carolina and have traveled a good bit, you're probably familiar with the differences between traditional North Carolina barbecue and what's served in other states or regions. But for those who have moved to North Carolina from elsewhere, as well as those Tar Heels who haven't ventured far outside our borders, some comparisons with other customs and practices may be helpful. If you're a true enthusiast, one of the most enjoyable parts of the entire barbecue mystique is to be able to "speak the lingo" wherever you travel; and in barbecue, as in everything, there's nothing like travel to give you a new appreciation of what you have at home.

For a preview of what awaits, you may want to think of barbecue spreading out from its origins in coastal Virginia and North Carolina more or less westward and southward, like a bucket of water sloshed onto the pavement. Now picture this tide having reached its limit at the southern and western United States borders, then flowing back toward North Carolina, bringing with it much of what it has picked up along the way. Today in North Carolina's cities and suburbs, there are barbecue restaurants serving not only pork in a thick, sweet, non-native barbecue sauce, but also beef, ribs, and even chicken—imports from other open-pit cuisines that have become a permanent part of our culture. There are actually a lot of recently transplanted North Carolina residents who don't even really understand the difference between the pit-cooked, chopped pork that's our traditional form of barbecue and these other variations. (A business executive who had recently transferred from Seattle was observed in Durham not long ago eyeing a tray of chopped North Carolina barbecue and asking a companion, "What's that gray meat?") In fact, most of us who do know the difference still occasionally enjoy eating beef, ribs, or chicken, heavily smoked and slathered with thick, dark red, sweet-hot sauce. And if we go into a grocery store to pick up barbecue sauce, we almost always reach for the thick, gooey kind. To us, this barbecue and *real* barbecue are two entirely different things, and we can hardly blame newcomers for being a little confused.

By way of clearing up some of this confusion, we'll go over some of the regional peculiarities you'll find as you travel across the southern United States—where nearly all the good barbecue is located. First, though, a general observation may be helpful. While most people automatically think *smoke* when they think of barbecue, there is a significant difference between the light smoking directly over hardwood coals given most North Carolina barbecue and the heavy doses of smoke administered to barbecued meat just about everywhere else. In Texas, and in dozens of states that have copied its barbecue, beef brisket, for example, is supposed to come off the pit smoked to a deep, blackish brown. This is generally accomplished either by cooking the meat over indirect heat, in some type of smoke chamber, or by using soaked wood chunks or green wood in combination with hardwood coals or placed atop electric coils. Slicing the meat is supposed to reveal a "smoke ring" encircling the brisket on all sides—a one-eighth-inch layer of dark pink or red just below the crusty brown edge, which is caused by the smoke seeping inside the meat. The smoky taste and aroma is so overpowering that a strong, sweet sauce is needed to balance the flavor and moisten the meat, which is usually somewhat dry. This combination of heavily smoked meat and sweet, thick sauce is probably what a majority of Americans think of as barbecue, and aspects of Texas-style barbecue have found their way into most of the regional barbecue variations you'll find in this country.

Here's a state-by-state rundown on what you might expect to find outside our borders.

North Carolina old-timers are fond of saying, "There's no more barbecue when you reach Virginia." That isn't 100-percent accurate, but it's true enough that you shouldn't worry yourself with learning about Virginia's barbecue practices—because there are practically none. It's a pity, but Virginians are obviously still being made to suffer for William Byrd's snide remark in 1728 that North Carolinians were full of "gross humors" from devouring so much swine's flesh. End of discussion.

South Carolina, on the other hand, has a lot of barbecue—some of it whole-hog, some from shoulders. There are quite a few places around the edges of the state that serve tasty sliced or pork-shoulder barbecue with a slightly thicker version of the tangy, Lexington-style sauce. However, the center of South Carolina, around Columbia, is the home of the Palmetto State's most notable barbecue peculiarity: mustard-based sauce. Ranging in color from a startling bright yellow to dull orange, this sauce features either honey or sugar to cut the mustard's pungency, plus vinegar, salt, peppers, spices, and sometimes catsup. The best places do a fine job of slow cooking over hardwood coals, so your biggest challenge to enjoying this barbecue variety may be a visual one: seeing the meat turned yellow by the sauce. The other South Carolina specialty, found virtually nowhere else, is barbecue hash, which is also known variously as pork hash or liver hash. Served over rice as a popular accompaniment to pork barbecue, this is a thick, meaty gravy which was devised to use up the organ meats that aren't cooked as barbecue. Brunswick stew is also common in the coastal regions of South Carolina.

Georgia, Alabama, and Tennessee all mainly serve pork barbecue, with some beef on the side, but pork ribs in these states are as much in demand as the meat from pork shoulders or hams. If it isn't clinging to a rib, most of the meat is sliced or pulled from shoulders and coated with a thick, red sauce ranging from mild to hot. (Not content with *tang*, Ridgewood Barbecue, one of the few outstanding spots in east Tennessee, brags that its sauce "has a *whang* to it.") Brunswick stew as a side dish is still fairly common in Georgia, although it's found only occasionally in northern Alabama and practically never in Tennessee.

Memphis merits special mention because it's home to the immense "Memphis in May" barbecue festival, featuring thousands of hungry visitors and hundreds of teams competing for cooking honors in the barbecuing of whole hogs, shoulders, and pork ribs. Heavy smoking and thick, tangy sauce are the order of the day, not only at the festival, but also at nearly a hundred Memphis barbecue restaurants that primarily serve shoulders and ribs. We should note that Memphians can choose from wet ribs (heavily sauced) or dry ribs,

A North Carolina Barbecue Primer

which are rubbed before cooking with a mixture of ground pepper and other spices then slow cooked over coals. While sauce is served on the side, a lot of folks enjoy the dry ribs with no adornment at all.

Of all the states in the Union, Kentucky probably has the oddest-sounding collection of barbecue customs, nearly all of them centered in the western end of the state just across the Ohio River from Illinois and Indiana. As strange as they may seem to us, most of these practices have been around since the 1830s. In the vicinity of Owensboro, which fancies itself the "Bar-B-Q Capital of the World," mutton—the meat of mature sheep—is far and away the most popular type of barbecue, and it has been for nearly 170 years due to the prevalence of sheep farming in the area in the early nineteenth century. Various Catholic parishes largely have been responsible for keeping this unique barbecued meat popular, originally holding mutton barbecues as social gatherings and, more recently, as fundraisers. Whole sheep are cut into quarters and slow roasted over hickory coals for up to sixteen hours, after which the meat is served sliced, either plain or graced by one of three possible sauces: mild tomato-based, "black dip" (heavily influenced by Worcestershire), or pepper-hot. Coleslaw is not considered a fit topping for a barbecue sandwich here; instead they're served with a slice of onion and a pickle. The most popular side dish is Burgoo, a spicy stew similar to Brunswick Stew, but also containing chopped mutton. (No one seems to know where this originated.) Owensboro holds a large barbecue festival each May, sometimes called "the burning of Owensboro" and featuring cinder-block barbecue pits built down the middle of a street running alongside the Ohio River.

Arkansas is a state with a distinct east-west barbecue orientation. In the east, pork is the most popular, with the attention more or less evenly split between shoulders and ribs. Western Arkansas, closest to Texas, is better known for its barbecued beef brisket. Thick, red sauce, with a kick to it, is served on all three barbecue varieties.

Texas, as we've already discussed, concerns itself mostly with beef brisket, although there is also quite a fondness for pit-smoked pork-sausage links. Pork shoulders and chicken are also found occasionally, and I've even been to places in Texas that offered barbecued duck. My impression at the time was that it didn't much matter what kind of meat you ordered: it all came to the table smoked to a deep rose hue and tasting about the same under the sweet, hot sauce. I've also had Texas sauce that wasn't as sweet—almost a gravy, flavored with more with chili pepper and cumin than catsup and molasses. Beans, both traditional baked beans and ranch-style pintos, are popular in Texas as a barbecue side dish. If cole-

NORTH CAROLINA BARBECUE : *Flavored by Time*

slaw is served, it will be the creamy variety, with lots of mayonnaise and sugar. Bread offered in accompaniment to the barbecue ranges from thick, grilled "Texas toast" to slices of plain loaf bread.

As I've said, I occasionally indulge in the heavily smoked and thickly sauced varieties of barbecue favored in other states, but my taste buds always feel vaguely hung over afterwards. To me, the difference between these versions and the real, traditional North Carolina barbecue is much like the difference between a woman masked by makeup and a lovely, fresh-faced young girl. Here at home, the tenderness and sweet, delicate taste of the pork itself is at the heart of the matter, and very little adornment in the way of heavy smoke or sauce is needed to enhance its natural appeal.

Serving guests at an eastern pig picking

Outside the Restaurant:
Pig Pickings, Contests, and *The* Festival

▞▞▞ Properly explaining North Carolina barbecue to an out-of-stater can be a tricky business. Once you've managed to establish the difference between traditional North Carolina barbecue and the oversmoked stuff doused with thick, red, sweet sauce that's called barbecue nearly everywhere today—including some places in our own state—and once you've dealt with the subtle but significant differences between our eastern and piedmont styles, you still really ought to make it clear to the uninitiated that there is yet another distinct stra-

tum of barbecue lore and enthusiasm in North Carolina. It can be called the "pig picking" culture, and its adherents are those thousands of Tar Heels who enjoy not only eating but cooking barbecue, and who enjoy barbecued pork served directly from someone's grill as much as they like the barbecue found in restaurants, if not more.

North Carolinians were attending barbecues long before there were any commercial barbecue stands or restaurants. Whether these events were held as purely social occasions, or perhaps to celebrate the "putting in" of a tobacco crop, the host would have someone chop the barbecued meat and serve it to his guests, along with corn bread, boiled potatoes, and other dishes. Catered barbecue buffets are still the order of the day at large meetings and political gatherings, while large barbecues at which the members prepare and serve the meat and the fixings themselves are popular fundraising events for churches and civic organizations. These larger events typically serve chopped barbecue, while the smaller, private barbecue has largely evolved into a more casual event that yesteryear's host might have considered downright barbaric: the pig picking.

Whereas hosts of old wouldn't have laid out a barbecued pig and expected the guests to pick or pull the meat from the bones with their fingers, pig-picking guests who are so inclined are invited to do just that. As a courtesy, most hosts will make sure a quantity of meat has already been pulled from the pig and chopped, ready to be served to those who don't want to roll up their sleeves and dive in. But to most folks, the very best part of a pig picking is finding and pulling the most delectable morsels of cooked pork from the pig—and the irresistible nibbling of shreds from the well-browned "crust" of the meat usually begins among the cooks even before the guests arrive.

No one knows exactly why pig pickings evolved (or devolved) from their more refined origins except that they obviously reflect a widespread trend toward a more casual approach to all types of entertaining. Judging by the name alone, an outsider might consider a pig picking an event designed by and for lowbrows, but nothing could be further from the truth. Remember, there is a reverse snobbery at work in barbecue circles, and it makes pig pickings equally popular among junior leaguers and farmers, blue-collar workers and lawyers. (Politicians can't resist them either.) When they're spiffed up a bit to include cloth napkins and china plates instead of paper and plastic, pig pickings are increasingly popular at wedding rehearsal dinners and even informal wedding receptions; while in their casual attire, they have long been a staple of reunions, church picnics, homecomings, and beer blasts.

In the North Carolina piedmont, where restaurant-barbecue universally comes from pork shoulders, the cooking of whole hogs for parties is relatively unusual, so the pig picking is essentially a ritual of the coastal plain. After all, the whole pig—cooked to a perfect golden brown and laid out on the grill for all to admire—is the star of the show, so a barbecue featuring several cooked pork shoulders just wouldn't be quite as appealing, at least from a visual standpoint. However, it is not uncommon for groups of men in the piedmont to organize a party around the all-night or all-day barbecuing of large

NORTH CAROLINA BARBECUE : *Flavored by Time*

quantities of pork shoulders—although the meat from these parties is nearly always sold for fundraising purposes rather than consumed on the spot.

At a down-east pig picking, the cooked pig is typically left spread out belly-up on the cooking grate, just as it was arranged during the last third of the cooking, so guests can pass by and serve themselves. The portions that disappear the fastest are the tenderloin—strips of lean, white meat on either side of the backbone—and the ribs; but to my taste, the firm, brown outside meat of the shoulders is hard to beat. Once guests have pulled off an appetizing serving of meat, they'll typically splash on a little tangy, vinegar-based sauce and fill up the remainder of their plate with coleslaw, boiled potatoes or Brunswick stew, and hush puppies, perhaps fresh fried on the spot.

My own awareness of events like pig pickings was born when I married a farm girl from Halifax County, the former Ruthie Everett of Palmyra. Although both my parents grew up in the eastern North Carolina hamlet of Newport—today the pig cooking-est town in the state—my father left home and became a Navy pilot, so I spent my growing-up years first in Florida, then later in the northern Virginia suburbs of Washington, D.C. On family visits to North Carolina, we would occasionally accompany my aunt, Meta Peters, to Bob Melton's ramshackle old bar-

becue place in Rocky Mount, but I never thought much about pigs, on or off the pit, until I married into a family that not only raised hogs but cooked them as well.

One of my earliest encounters with my future father-in-law should have made it clear to me that pigs had a place in my future. Ruthie and I met and fell in love while we were both students at UNC-Chapel Hill, and when I drove to her family's large farm near Scotland Neck so we could jointly inform her parents of our plans to marry, I ended up declaring my intentions to Fate Everett smack in the middle of a pig parlor containing hundreds of malodorous, loudly squealing hogs. Ruthie had tipped him off as to why I was there, so when I stammered out something along the lines of, "Um, I, uh, love your daughter and I, uh, want to marry her," he pretended not to be able to hear me over the deafening racket. Cupping his hand behind his ear, he made me keep repeating myself until, straining to be heard above the insistent hogs, I screamed at the top of my lungs: "I LOVE YOUR DAUGHTER AND I WANT TO MARRY HER!" Finally, a grin broke across his face, and clapping me on the shoulder, he offered me a cigar. In great relief, I accepted and puffed clumsily away, squinting through the smoke as though I were a seasoned old pig farmer.

Several months later, Ruthie's father and two brothers, Bob and Tad, threw a pig picking for me at my bachelor party. I believe it was the first pig picking I'd ever attended, and I have a dim recollection of a huge old pair of (freshly laundered) women's drawers wrapped and tied around a stick to make a mop for basting sauce onto the pig. The liquid refreshments were flowing freely that night, though, and after twenty-seven years, my only other recollection of the all-male event is that my best man Ed Stoddard and I became swept up in a spirit of oratory and recited an earthy poem dressed in nothing but athletic supporters, after which we "mooned" the entire assembly.

Following our marriage, Ruthie and I lived in Denver, Colorado, for two years, then moved back to North Carolina, where we settled first in Chapel Hill and later in Greensboro, a couple of hours away from her parents' home. Although we had our circle of Greensboro friends, getting together with young couples from Scotland Neck, including Ruthie's brother, Tad, and his wife Jayne, to "cook a pig" at the farm became a popular weekend social event, especially since none of us had much money and the nearest movie theater or nice restaurant was thirty miles away. (We also didn't have to pay for the pigs.)

My other brother-in-law, Bob Everett, was living and working in Georgia at the time, following his graduation from North Carolina State University, so it was Tad who began to introduce me to the all-day process of cooking a pig.

On one occasion, Tad threw a dressed hog in the trunk of his car and drove up to Greensboro to help me put on a pig picking for my newsroom coworkers at WFMY-TV. I remember that he struggled mightily to get the pig fully cooked on a makeshift, outdoor pit, and I recall all of us singing "Shall We Gather At The River" in tipsy hilarity as we passed the hat to cover the costs of the meal. I remember that we didn't collect enough the first time around, so we passed the hat (and perhaps a bottle) a second time while singing another verse.

Most of those early pig pickings, though, were at the farm, where Tad, who's also a N.C. State graduate, lived with his wife and farmed with his father. He was equipped with what at the time was considered a fancy trailer-cooker made from a large oil tank. Having slaughtered, cleaned, and dressed a hog the previous evening, we would fire up the cooker with the first bath of glowing coals and get the pig on the grate, meat-side down, early on a Saturday morning, spreading the coals evenly across the bottom of the cooker. For the remainder of the morning, in between adding some fresh coals every hour or so, we usually occupied ourselves with preparing the sauce or making coleslaw, and an hour or so before noon, we would usually throw some

NORTH CAROLINA BARBECUE : *Flavored by Time*

venison steaks on the cooker next to the pig so they would be ready for lunch.

After the average-sized pig had cooked meat-side-down for around six hours, it was time to turn it over. This was always an occasion for anxiety because it plainly revealed how well you had done the first half of your job. The idea was to perfectly brown the meat without charring it, a task you had to try to accomplish without being able to see what you were doing since the meat was facing downward. If you had spread too many coals under the roasting pig, you might turn it to find that it had burned, in which case you knew the clear evidence of your lack of skill would be lying there for all the world to see. In order to avoid this embarrassment, you had to try to control the heat and the rate of browning by avoiding adding too many coals at once; by being careful to keep them spread in a single layer, never having one coal lying atop another; and by spreading additional coals only under the thicker ham and shoulder portions. In fact, after having spread the original layers of coals, we never added any more to the center area under the ribs and loin. We used eyes and ears and fingers to judge whether the temperature was about right: as long as we could put an ear next to the cooker and hear the hissing of fat dripping onto the hot coals, lay our fingers on top of the cooker and leave them there for a second or two, and see a faint whisp of smoke coming out of the stack, we knew we were all right. Heavy smoke or a cooker too hot to the touch, on the other hand, was a sure sign that you had probably added too many coals, and that the pig would be charred if you didn't quickly close all the air vents and get the fire dampened down.

Turning the pig was a matter of placing a second rectangular wire grate, identical to the first, on *top* of the split hog and, with a man on each corner, firmly squeezing together the handles of both the top and bottom grates, turning the "sandwiched" pig so that the skin side now rested over the coals. If properly done, the meat-side-down cooking period had not only browned the pig to perfection, but had gotten the pig at least three-quarters done. The only remaining jobs were allowing the meat to slowly finish cooking as the skin browned and occasionally basting the meat with sauce.

The hours between the early to midafternoon turning of the pig and the serving of dinner around six were likely to be mischief filled. You must understand that cooking a pig is a very drawn-out undertaking, with occasional spurts of activity punctuating long periods of sitting around with little to do. As such, it's a perfect way for men to spend a day socializing with their friends and neighbors, and there's always plenty of yarn spinning; discussing of farming, sports, or politics; and other forms of sociability. It is not unknown, once afternoon arrives, for the participants to "take a drink" as they visit with one another and keep an eye on the cooking pig.

In those newly married days, our callowness and sense of youthful invincibility sometimes allowed our own pig cooking gatherings to get a little out of hand. On one Saturday, after "taking" one drink too many, several of us ended up challenging each other to a shooting contest. Standing in a nearby pasture, one of us would toss his cap high in the air and a challenger would try to blast it with a shotgun. (The fact that someone might easily have been hurt or killed makes me shudder as I recall the incident.) Another time found a light rain beginning to fall just as guests were beginning to help themselves to the pig. Undaunted (and well lubricated by an afternoon of socializing), we pushed the cooker up the back porch, picked up the entire grill, and regally bore the cooked pig into the house, setting it down on a huge butcher-block table in the kitchen. My brother-in-law Bob was living in the family homeplace as a bachelor at the time, following the death of his mother and the remarriage of his father; otherwise, we never would have either considered or gotten away with such a thing. A lively indoor pig picking and party ensued. However, we all bit-

terly regretted our foolishness the next day, as we nursed our hangovers while scrubbing massive deposits of greasy hog drippings from the kitchen floor.

As my young children began to be more aware of their surroundings (and I began to grow up a bit, too), I decided that my own family would be happier and more stable in an alcohol-free environment, so my youthful partying came to an end. My enjoyment of pig pickings, however, continued unabated. Playing at being a gentleman farmer, I had moved to a large, old house in the countryside near Burlington, and had even acquired my own pig cooker. Although I never did any catering, I often organized pig pickings for groups of friends, Sunday-school classes, my sons' Boy Scout troop, and even a group of kids from Belfast, Northern Ireland, who were spending a summer in Greensboro.

One sweltering July evening, I pulled into the driveway with the cooker in tow, a freshly dressed pig already spread-eagled on the grill. The pig was to be cooked the following day. . . . But where could I keep the meat cool in the meantime? Since then, I have learned to slide a dressed pig into a new, large, rubber garbage can and to pack bags of ice around it, but at the time, the only thing I could think to do was to lay the hog out on the floor of my cellar, the coolest spot in the house. Having no one to help me, I managed to get the pig onto a sheet of

NORTH CAROLINA BARBECUE : *Flavored by Time*

clear, heavy plastic and pull the sheet and its heavy load down a short flight of steps to the basement, where I wrapped the plastic around the pig and covered it with bags of ice.

The next morning, anxious to get the pig onto the fire, I discovered in desperation that I couldn't drag the plastic sheet back up the cellar steps without having the pig slide off onto the floor. I had already sawed off the slender "trotters" so the pig would fit into the cooker, and when I tried to grasp the stumpy legs, my hands slid right off the smooth, clammy skin. Even if I had been able to hoist the 130-pound form onto my shoulder, the cellar ceiling was too low to stand upright or even get higher than a back-breaking crouch. Pondering the true meaning of the term "dead weight," I finally had an inspiration. Getting down on my knees, I was able to get the pig's front legs up over my shoulders, and holding the inert hog to my body with both arms, I struggled to my feet. Looking for all the world like an exhausted marathon dancer, I hugged that lifeless pig for all I was worth as I stumbled backwards up the stairs and into the early morning sunlight. Unfortunately, not having thought far enough ahead, I found myself with an armful of cold pig and no clear idea of what to do next. Attempting to rest the front legs on the edge of a table and slither down the pig's body to the back legs so I could shove the

whole thing safely onto the flat surface, I dropped the pig, meat-side down, onto the ground. For the next two hours, I picked grass, twigs, and bits of soil from the tacky surface of the exposed meat, swearing all the while that this would be the last pig I ever cooked.

It wasn't, though, and I've both organized and attended dozens more pig pickings since then—all strictly for fun. However, for many barbecue cooks, the pig pickings that began as a way to pass Saturdays leisurely have been replaced by extremely competitive cooking contests, imbued with great seriousness of purpose. Although any of these pig cooking hobbyists will tell you that the competition *is* great fun, there's a lot of hard work, time, and expense involved, balanced somewhat by the potential for winning big-time cash prizes.

North Carolina now has some twenty-five whole-hog cooking contests of various sizes, but the field is totally dominated by chefs from the coastal plain, where cooking whole pigs, rather than shoulders, has long been the norm. In fact, twenty-two of the twenty-five pork cook-offs are held east of Raleigh, and two more take place in Hillsborough and Burlington, which are located more or less on an indistinct line between east and piedmont in terms of barbecue customs. Tryon, North Carolina, located near the South Carolina line at the foot of the Blue Ridge Mountains, has one of only a few annual barbecue-cooking contests anywhere in the western half of the state, and it's really a hybrid affair, featuring a little North Carolina barbecue but also a lot of ribs, beef, and chicken in the thick-sauce-and-heavy-smoke style found from Tennessee westward. The Tryon festival is only three years old, but for the third consecutive year, organizers have pulled political strings to have it designated by the governor's office as the Official North Carolina State Barbecue Championship. Since most of the Tryon competitors are from out of state, that rather grand designation hopefully will not cause this new event to be mistaken for the North Carolina Championship Pork Cook-Off, the whole-hog state contest held each year by the North Carolina Pork Producers Association—with entrance open only to winners of various local pig-cooking contests in North Carolina. (The state contest and many of the local cook-offs are now judged under a standard set of criteria developed by the association.)

Because potential contestants have been eliminated in earlier contests, the state cook-off normally has a field of only forty or so cooking teams, whereas the biggest contest of all is one of the local affairs, the renowned Newport Pig Cookin' Contest. Located in flat, sandy Carteret County, Newport is a small tobacco town and bedroom community for the nearby Cherry Point Marine Air Station at Havelock. However, during the last twenty-five years or so, it has become famous as the spot where more than one hundred pig-cooking teams gather to compete for barbecue bragging rights and prizes. During the '50s and early '60s, when I was occasionally visiting maternal and paternal grandparents in Newport, I don't recall ever seeing an entire pig barbecued, or even hearing of such a practice, but the festival later grew from tiny beginnings into a massive event in which a majority of townspeople participate as volunteers. Profits derived from contest entry fees are used for a wide range of civic purposes.

Whereas most pig pickings used to feature hogs roasted over coals in cookers made from oil tanks, most of today's competitive pig-cooking teams use sleek, custom-made grills—many of them heated by gas. Proponents of gas cooking say the fuel allows them to control temperatures precisely inside the cooker over a long period of time, which means they can cook a pig at a constant low temperature for up to twelve hours, producing extremely moist, tender meat. But among the latest additions, gas tanks are the least extravagant. Nearly all of the modern grills are outfitted with expensive thermometers, fancy hand or automatic systems for turning the pig, towel-and-utensil racks, cutting boards, smokestacks shaped like pigs, and dozens of other gadgets. Most of them receive gleaming new paint jobs, inside and out, before every contest, making them a far cry

NORTH CAROLINA BARBECUE : *Flavored by Time*

from the comfortably rusted cooker with the blackened lid that I'm used to.

In fact, if I were to enter a contest with that old cooker, I would be at a distinct disadvantage in cooking with hardwood or charcoal—not only because of the increased difficulty of maintaining an even, low temperature with hand-spread coals, but also because of the emphasis placed by judges on near perfection in appearance and cleanliness. Not only is the pig expected to be cooked to perfection, but the cooker, the surrounding area, *and the cook* are expected to remain virtually spotless throughout the process. Hardwood coals and charcoal produce fine ash, some of which ends up floating around the cooker, invariably coating the lid, the grill, and even the pig unless it's covered by cardboard or foil. At a pig picking, the chef can claim that any ash falling on the pig "makes it taste better" and can ignore the rest, but in a contest, the same ash would be a cause for points to be deducted. I'm delighted to know that these contests still are won occasionally by teams cooking with wood and charcoal, and I salute them for keeping the old ways alive.

When it comes down to judging the meat itself, the tiniest details of a cooked pig's appearance are scrutinized by hard-eyed judges and spectators alike. The pig is expected to be roasted to a uniform golden brown, and any charred spots on the meat, no matter how small, will set tongues clucking and scores tumbling. Should the soft, cooked meat separate from the bone or otherwise pull apart as the pig is being turned, the chef will have his score lowered accordingly. And if there are any unnecessary cuts on the meat—as might be made in testing for doneness—the cook can abandon any hope of being listed among the contest's winners. Daryll Garner, the longtime mayor of Newport (and a distant relative of mine), jokes about how the town's eye for pig judging may have clouded the community's reputation. The mayor swears he has heard out-of-staters saying, "They must have some ugly women around here . . . all I hear is, 'Have you seen that good-lookin' pig of Tom's? Well, no, but I have seen Harry's and *that's* a pretty pig.'"

The pork producers association holds an annual barbecue judges' school, at which prospective judges spend an entire afternoon viewing slides and video and poring over the criteria listed on score sheets. "What's wrong with this pig?," calls out expert-cooker Jim Ferrell of Newport, one of the school's instructors. Gazing at a blurry slide of a well-browned pig that's slightly blackened around the backbone and ribs, the judges-to-be sing out in unison: "It's burned!" For on-site judging, in which the judge visits each cooking location at a contest, the score sheets guide the judges in awarding the cooked pig from between two to forty points in six categories covering appearance and taste. But before the evaluation actually even begins, the judge has to answer a crucial question written at the top of the first sheet: "Is this pig done?" If judges determine that the pig is *not* completely cooked, the entry is immediately disqualified.

In the on-site evaluation, it's ironic that the judges' job is to approach a cooked pig, with nary a word to the anxious chef, and tear it to pieces as quickly as they can. One judge will lift the pig and begin stabbing it from underneath with a large knife, probing for soft spots in what is supposed to be a uniformly crisp skin. Others, wearing rubber gloves, will thrust their hands into the cooked meat, tossing chunks here and there as they test for doneness and texture. Grabbing a bit of meat from the tenderloin, the judges will dunk it into a waiting bowl of sauce and impassively take a bite, avoiding any telltale facial expression as they jot down their scores. In a few moments, it's all over and they move on to the next entry, leaving the stunned cook gazing dolefully at the scattered remains of what had been a really *pretty* pig.

Once the damage has been done, however, the meat is chopped and seasoned and submitted for a blind taste test, which accounts for a third of the total score. A well-known contestant—perhaps a former champion— could conceivably receive higher scores in the on-site judging purely because of his reputation, but a blind taste test is supposed to help balance such potential inequities since each entry is identified only by number and not by name.

Contestants are even graded on showmanship. Many teams erect elaborate sets around their cookers: a tobacco-barn scene, for example, or a country kitchen, and team members are often in costume. The cooks are supposed to demonstrate that they're having a good time and to be "good will ambassadors for pork."

While the fiercely competitive eastern North Carolina pig-cooking contests often serve as centerpieces for community-wide celebrations, the state's largest and most successful barbecue festival represents something of a temporary cease-fire among competitors. Bringing together top Lexington-style barbecue restaurateurs to serve their trademark pork shoulder barbecue under a common banner, the Lexington Barbecue Festival is actually a re-creation of an earlier type of event, one that helped begin this piedmont town's barbecue heritage. In the early 1900s, public cook-outs, known as "Everybody's Day," helped introduce barbecue to the folks around Lexington, fanning embers of enthusiasm that later burst into the hot flames of passion. It wasn't long before these occasional barbecues were expanded into week-long events designed to serve the crowds attending court sessions, and by 1919, Sid Weaver

Different types of cookers used in pig-cooking contests

Up to 150,000 people attend the Lexington Barbecue Festival

and George Ridenhour had set up their first barbecue stand, a stone's throw from the Davidson County courthouse. These week-long festivals eventually disappeared, but in 1984, the concept of an "Everybody's Day"— a community-wide celebration of Lexington's legendary barbecue style—was brought back in an expanded form. And since that time, it has attracted visitors in ever-increasing numbers from all over the Southeast.

Lexington, located off Interstate 85 between Greensboro and Charlotte, is a town of some 17,000 people, but it has, at last count, twenty barbecue restaurants. According to Greg Johnson and Vince Staton's fine book, *Real Barbecue*, Lexington is second among the nation's cities in terms of barbecue restaurants per capita, with one barbecue place for every 850 residents. (Ironically, Lexington, Tennessee, with ten restaurants to serve 6,000 residents, was in first place.) Obviously, there is a large enough pie in Lexington for all the barbecuers to have a slice, and a handful of the top restaurant owners organized the first barbecue festival around the principal of minimizing their differences and promoting Lexington-style barbecue as a distinctive regional delicacy.

Lexington's barbecue festival is traditionally held on one of the last two Saturdays in October, but as a warmup to the big event, the entire month has been designated "Barbecue

Month." Not content with the time constraints of a one-day festival, organizers fill the October calendar with events such as the Tour de Pig (a cycling race); a three-mile Hawg Run; a beauty pageant; golf, tennis, and softball tournaments; and, so help me, a Barbecue Cheer-Off.

On the morning of the big day, the festivities get underway with the Parade of Pigs. Lest you immediately get a mental image (as I did) of hundreds of unfortunate pigs being herded down Main Street toward their doom by broom-wielding citizens, be reassured that organizers describe the parade as consisting of "a variety of floats and people carrying out the pork-flavor theme." For the festival, a seven-block stretch of Main Street is closed to traffic, and some four hundred exhibitors set up shop, selling everything from crafts to homemade fudge. There is musical entertainment throughout the festival, including a concert or two by headline acts, as well as a juried art competition and show, a carnival midway, a classic car show, and an area with rides and entertainment for children called "Piglet Land."

In 1995, some of the literal *and* figurative distance between east and piedmont was bridged when the state pork producers association voted to accept the city's invitation for the annual North Carolina Championship Pork Cook-Off to be held in Lexington in conjunction with the Lexington Barbe-

Donnie Roberts

Cheer-Off contestants in Lexington
Courtesy Lexington Dispatch

cue Festival. Piedmont residents, used to seeing pits full of pork shoulders, were able to watch the state's top whole-hog cooking experts—nearly all of them from the coastal plain—demonstrate their craft.

The real festival action, though, is always under three large red-and-white-striped tents on the courthouse square—tents somewhat reminiscent of those early shelters set up by

Sid Weaver and Jess Swicegood. Here, genuine Lexington-style chopped barbecue sandwiches, slaw, and french fries are served at a furious rate by volunteers and restaurant workers, many of whom also spend the two days prior to the event cooking some twelve thousand extra pounds of pork shoulders to feed the expected 100,000-plus in attendance.

Just as rail travel through places like Lexington and Salisbury once helped spread barbecue's reputation, the Lexington Barbecue Festival of today is crucial in maintaining Lexington's standing around piedmont and western North Carolina as a barbecue mecca. The main section of Interstate 85 between Charlotte and Greensboro now bypasses the city several miles to the east, which means the average traveler has to have a specific reason for going into Lexington. Heavy television and newspaper coverage of the festival each year helps maintain the visibility of the town's twenty barbecue restaurants and gives a passerby all the reason he or she needs to take the Lexington exit.

To North Carolinians, contests and festivals are an important way of keeping old customs alive, as evidenced by the large crowds attending such disparate North Carolina events as the annual hollerin' contest, the coastal duck decoy festival, and the mountain festival honoring the ramp, a pungent cousin to the onion. The Lexington Barbecue Festival and the dozens of barbecue contests scattered around the state certainly help keep North Carolina's premier ethnic food in the public eye. The state pork producer's association has had a barbecue task force for the past several years, with the aim of not only promoting contests and festivals, but also popularizing pig pickings as a fashionably casual way of re-encountering barbecue up close and personal. Over the past few years, barbecue may have lost a few popularity points to grilled chicken breasts or taco salads or whatever as a frequent menu choice, but as a savory symbol of North Carolina's rural heritage, it's as popular and visible as it ever was—and that's largely due to its having been celebrated so widely and so often.

Pork Shoulder or Whole Hog:
How to Prepare Your Own North Carolina Barbecue

■▬■▬■ Barbecue is like a coquettish young woman, favoring only those suitors who ply her with considerable time and attention. Most of us, busy with our everyday lives, pay someone else to spend the long, hot hours required to prepare good barbecue—to carry on the dalliance, if you will—so that we can simply show up at the last minute and reap the rewards. But there are at least a couple of reasons that you occasionally might want to invest some time preparing your own barbecue.

The first is that barbecue is at its absolute peak of perfection when it's pulled straight off the bone, still steaming hot from the pit. Morsels of pork—reddish brown and crusty, creamy white and bursting with just-released juices, or cocoa hued and sweetly tender—will never again delight the senses in exactly the same way as when the bewitching, aromatic vapors from juices hissing onto hot coals rise swirling and wafting around the moist, succulent meat like a cloud of smiling attendants inviting the guests to the banquet table. Of course, it is remotely possible to enjoy barbecue this perfect in a restaurant—

provided that you show up just as it's being freshly chopped, and providing that the fresh batch is intended to be served at once, which is seldom the case. On the other hand, even the best places find it difficult to hold barbecue at its most tender, flavorful point when it has to be kept warm over a period of time.

The other, more important reason—particularly for men—is that the very process of slow-cooking barbecue is a perfect focal point for a day of leisure in the company of others, especially since it also provides a superb meal to be shared at the end of the day. Barbecuing a pork shoulder in a backyard grill can engage the attention of one or two persons for much of a day, while cooking an entire pig is an undertaking suited to a slightly larger group.

Across the rural areas of eastern North Carolina, the all-day ritual of roasting a pig provides a setting for small groups of men to tell jokes, hold serious discussions on the issues of the day . . . even do some sociable tippling. And even among those who don't live in the country, barbecuing a pig is a wonderful way for a group of fast friends to spend a day together. But preparing a pig picking can also provide a great social framework for getting acquainted with people you don't really know. Many of those who live in suburban neighborhoods are so engrossed with the details of jobs and child rearing that they hardly know their neighbors up and

down the street, but throwing a pig picking is a surefire way to remedy that situation. You can choose four or five men and spend the day getting to know one another through the sharing of a task, all the while preparing a feast for a group of fifty or more. The details involved in actually cooking the pig will provide plenty of conversational material and help bridge any awkward lulls, while the minor mistakes and mishaps that are bound to occur will help cement your budding relationships with laughter. You may decide to furnish the entire meal, getting several people to help you with side dishes such as coleslaw or hush puppies; you might opt to purchase these accompaniments from a restaurant—or you may simply turn the event into a covered-dish buffet, with guests bringing their favorite side dishes and desserts. In any case, the guests will enjoy making a fuss over the gloriously roasted entrée, and you'll be assured of having pulled off a successful party.

If you would prefer to spend a quiet Saturday with your family or a friend or two, barbecuing a pork shoulder in an ordinary covered grill is a low-stress, day-long activity that leaves plenty of time for visiting and puttering, and provides enough meat to invite several couples over for dinner at the end of the day.

Whether you cook a single shoulder or the entire pig, the barbecue will be as good as any you've ever had in your life—and you'll have very pleasant memories of the day you spent preparing it.

Cooking a Pork Shoulder

While this is a process that doesn't require much work, it does take a good deal of time, so if you want to serve dinner at 6:00 P.M., you'll need to get started by 9:00 in the morning. You'll either need a six- to seven-pound fresh shoulder picnic or Boston Butt (the two halves cut from the twelve- to fifteen-pound whole shoulder, which is what's barbecued by restaurants); a covered, kettle-type grill; ten pounds of high quality hard-wood charcoal (I prefer Kingsford); a bag of hickory wood *chunks* (not chips); a second grill or other container for lighting additional coals; a small shovel or scoop; and a pair of heavy-duty rubber gloves.

Begin by generously salting the exposed-meat side of the picnic or Boston Butt and leave it out at room temperature for thirty minutes or so while you're getting the charcoal fire ready. Light five pounds of charcoal in the bottom of the grill and wait until the briquettes are entirely covered with gray ash. When the coals are ready, leave six or seven briquettes in a ten-inch circle at the center of the grill and push the remaining briquettes into two even piles on opposite sides of the grill. Gently place two hickory chunks on

Everett Garner

Fresh Boston Butt barbecued on kettle-type grill

Everett Garner

Add 6 briquettes through the grate's side openings every 30 minutes.

Everett Garner

Drop two hickory chunks on top of fresh briquettes.

top of each pile, being careful not to collapse the mound of briquettes. When the chunks begin to smoke, put the wire cooking grate in place and set the shoulder on it, directly over the circle of coals in the center. Place the meat side down so that the fat can drip all the way down through the meat and onto the coals (this keeps the meat from drying out). Place the cover on the grill, leaving the ventilation holes completely open.

(Note: When working with a charcoal fire this small, I've found that hickory wood chips don't work very well. If you soak them in water for thirty minutes, as the manufacturer recommends, they often kill the coals when they are placed on the fire, whereas if you put them atop the briquettes without soaking, they tend to catch fire, causing excessive darkening and drying of the meat. The larger chunks, on the other hand, are slow to burst into flame and usually provide a good thirty minutes of smoke before they need replacing. You won't need to soak them, since they'll seldom burst flame up as long as the cover is on the grill.)

As soon as you have the meat on the fire, you'll need to light another pile of around twelve briquettes in your secondary grill or fire bucket so that they'll be ready to add to the grill in approximately thirty minutes. When the briquettes are completely covered with gray ash, transfer them to the grill, gently adding six briquettes to each pile. Some

kettle grills, such as the Weber brand, have an opening at each side of the wire cooking grate that allows you to add additional coals or wood chunks without removing the grate. Lay two more hickory chunks atop the fresh coals on each side, replacing the grill's lid as quickly as possible.

One of my favorite outdoor-cooking implements is a folding, army-surplus shovel or entrenching tool, which is ideal for transferring the lighted coals from one grill to the other. Actually, any small shovel or scoop will serve; a pair of barbecue tongs will also do the trick nicely, although tongs take a little longer since you can move only one briquette at a time.

Continue adding six fully lit briquettes and two hickory chunks to each side of the grill every thirty minutes or so. You won't need to add any more briquettes to the center, directly under the meat—the meat will become deeply browned without any additional coals in the center. In between the addition of fresh coals, try to resist the temptation to lift the lid to inspect the meat—this causes significant heat loss and slows down the cooking process.

Around 3:30 or 4:00 in the afternoon—or after about six hours on the grill—turn the picnic or Boston Butt so that the meat side is facing up. At this point, you can reduce the number of coals to four or five on each side if it looks as though the meat is brown-

NORTH CAROLINA BARBECUE : *Flavored by Time*

ing too quickly, but it's important to keep adding coals and wood chunks on a regular basis so that the temperature in the kettle grill doesn't get too low.

After another couple of hours of cooking with the skin side down, both the exposed meat and the skin of the shoulder should be a deep reddish brown. Put on your rubber gloves and give the meat a good squeeze with both hands; it should be done enough for you to feel the meat "give" beneath your fingers. Wearing the rubber gloves, transfer the shoulder from the grill to a pan or a cutting board. The skin covering one entire side of the shoulder should easily lift off in one piece with just a gentle tug. Set the skin aside and use a sharp knife to scrape or cut away any fat which may be clinging to the meat. The remaining lean meat should be tender enough for you to easily tear it off the bone in chunks by hand, although it's all right if you need to use a knife to finish the job.

Arrange the chunks of meat into a pile on the cutting board and chop the cooked pork to the consistency you like with a heavy cleaver. (You may prefer to either slice the meat or continue pulling it into smaller pieces with your fingers.) The meat should be liberally splashed with a sauce of your choice—a tart, vinegar-tomato, Lexington-style sauce would be appropriate—and served either on a plate accompanied by coleslaw or on a warm, soft bun topped with slaw.

Cooking an Entire Pig

Pig pickings are appropriate at any time of the year, although fall and spring are my favorite pig-cooking seasons.

The heat of a summer's day will cause the pig to finish cooking much more quickly, but after tending a hot cooker in these temperatures all day, you'll end up pretty well "done" yourself by the time dinner is served. Also, most people seem to eat a little more lightly in the summertime than is normal at a pig picking, and on the hot, humid summer evenings that are typical in North Carolina, getting anywhere near a heated cooker may be more than most people want to tackle. In the winter, the cold air circulating around the cooker saps the heat and may cause you to have difficulty getting the pig cooked all the way through, unless the cooking is done in a sheltered location. You'll also have to arrange to serve—or at least eat—inside once the cooking is done.

But the warm, gentle days and cool nights of autumn and spring are perfect for a pig picking, not only for providing a comfortable outdoor environment for cooking, but also for adding a bounce to your step and a keenness to your appetite. According to tradition, pigs were often roasted in autumn on pits dug under the overhanging shelters of tobacco barns, as farmers celebrated the harvesting and curing of their crop. So fall may be the *most* perfect time for a pig picking—but really, the perfect time comes whenever you have a hankering for some great barbecue and a day of pleasant company.

You can obtain a whole pig for barbecuing from a meat-packing house; a barbecue wholesaler; or a retail supermarket, although you'll want to check to see what kind of advance notice a supermarket requires: it generally ranges from three to seven days. If you're a pig-picking novice, a hog which "dresses out" at 75-80 pounds is an easy size to handle and will cook in seven hours. Since the general rule of thumb for feeding mixed male-and-female groups is to plan on one-and-a-half pounds of carcass weight per person, a 75- to 80-pound pig will feed a crowd of twenty-five couples, or a hungry, all-male group of around forty. By comparison, a 100-pound pig will cook in eight hours and feed a mixed group of sixty-five, while a 125-pound pig will take nine hours to cook and feed a mixed crowd of around eighty-five people. Don't become confused by the difference between a pig's weight "on the hoof" and the "dressed weight" you'll specify when you order; "dressed weight" means the pig will have been completely cleaned and scraped free of bristles, and that its head will have been removed.

(Note: If the cooker you'll be using has some provision for turning the pig during cooking, such as a double grate, you should specify that you want the pig delivered with the backbone split—so that the pig will lie flat on the grate, but with the skin left intact. Otherwise, I suggest that you have the supplier go ahead and cut the pig in half lengthwise, since the two separate halves will be fairly easy to turn by hand.)

There are a lot of fancy, custom-made pork cookers out there, most of which are designed for use in pig-cooking competitions. All you'll need, though, is a simple cooker of the type made from a 250-gallon oil tank mounted on a two-wheeled trailer. These are generally available for a reasonable rental charge at various locations around the state, and if you're having trouble finding a source, you might try asking the meat packer or grocer who's supplying your pig. (The perfect situation, of course, is to have a friend who will let you borrow his cooker.) Your cooker should be outfitted with a wire grate, a door cut into each end for adding additional coals and ventilation, and a smokestack. The rental agency will expect you to return the cooker in a reasonably clean condition, with the coals and ashes removed and the grate scraped clean of bits of meat and skin.

I use charcoal for cooking pigs. I know there are purists who insist that only wood coals can impart the right flavor to barbecued pork, while others swear by the precise temperature control that gas cookers provide. But I'm convinced that high-quality, hardwood charcoal briquettes, such as the ones made by Kingsford, provide just as much taste as wood coals. They also hold their heat much longer, meaning you need fewer coals and don't have to add them as frequently. (Gas is much easier and more precise but, in my opinion, adds no outdoor-cooked taste at all.) You'll need sixty pounds of charcoal for a 75- to 80-pound pig, seventy pounds of briquettes for a pig weighing 100 pounds, and eighty pounds of charcoal for a 125-pound pig.

In addition to a pig, a cooker, and charcoal, you'll need the following items for your pig picking: a kettle-type grill or other container for lighting additional coals, lighter fluid, a shovel and hoe for transferring and spreading coals, a table to hold your various supplies, paper towels, heavy-duty rubber gloves for handling the pork, a container for sauce and some sort of basting implement, a cleaver and a chopping block if you're planning to chop any of the barbecue, chairs for "kicking back," and your favorite cool beverages.

For a 75- to 80-pound pig that you want to serve at 6:00 P.M., you should get started by 9:00 in the morning; this allows a couple of hours more than the recommended seven-hour cooking time to cover setting up, organizing your supplies, and getting your first coals ready. It also gives you a little bit of a "fudge factor" in case you inadvertently let the coals go out, or have some other minor problem during the day. Begin by opening the cooker's lid, removing and setting aside the cooking grate, and placing a twenty-pound bag of charcoal so that it lies flat in the center of the cooker's floor. Rip open the entire top side of the bag and generously soak the briquettes with lighter fluid, giving the fluid a minute to soak in before you light the charcoal. Leave the lid open while the coals are burning down to their desired state.

While you're waiting on the coals, trim and discard any excess fat or unsightly scraps from the pig. You'll probably also want to use a saw to cut off the hooves, or "trotters," and get rid of the tail, since some guests don't appreciate any extraneous reminders of the pig's former existence as an actual barnyard animal. Using a large, sharp knife, make a couple of deep cuts parallel to the bone in the exposed-meat side of each shoulder or ham. (In a contest, these cuts would cause points to be deducted under the "appearance" category, but in the real world, most cooks believe they help ensure that these thickest parts of the pig get thoroughly cooked, right down to the bone.) Generously salt all the exposed meat.

When the briquettes in the cooker are all covered with gray ash, use a garden hoe to spread them out in an even layer across the

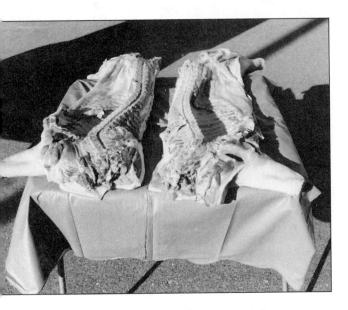

A whole pig is easier to turn if it's split in half.

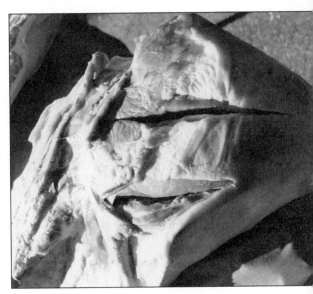

Deep cuts in hams and shoulders help ensure doneness.

To begin, soak entire bag of briquettes with charcoal lighter.

Lighted briquettes are transferred from ordinary grill, at left, to pig cooker.

5 lbs. of briquettes are spread beneath hams and shoulders every 45 minutes.

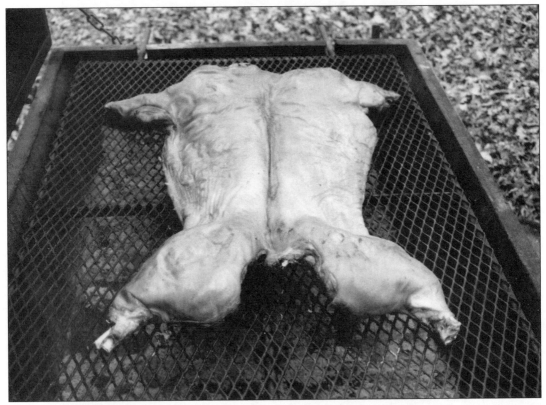

Pig roasts skin-side-up for first 6 hours.

Baste pig with sauce after it's turned.

entire floor of the cooker so that no coal is resting atop or touching another. Replace the cooking grate and have someone help you carry the pig to the cooker, placing it centered—skin side up—on the grate. Make sure the pig is lying flat, then close the lid.

Once the pig is on the grill, take a well-deserved break for a few minutes—then light another five pounds of charcoal in your secondary grill so that it will be ready to scatter under the pig about forty-five minutes after it was first placed on the cooker. Once this second batch of coals is ready, they should be divided evenly and scattered beneath the

hams and shoulders only; use a shovel and reach through the doors at each end of the cooker to spread the coals. No additional briquettes will be required under the center of the pig until it has been turned skin side down; if you add coals to this area before then, there's a good chance the rib area will be burned when you turn the pig over.

This same pattern is repeated over the course of the next five hours. Every forty-five minutes or so, five pounds of briquettes, covered with gray ash, should be spread evenly beneath the hams and shoulders. Periodically check the ventilation doors at each end of the cooker; normally they should be left cracked open by about an inch to allow for air circulation over the coals. Avoid lifting the lid to look at the cooking meat, because this causes much of the accumulated heat to be lost. The temperature inside the cooker should remain at a fairly constant level of about 225 degrees, but unlike some of the high-tech competition cookers, the one you'll be using probably won't have a thermometer, so you'll have to use your hand to estimate the temperature. You should be able to rest your palm on the cooker's closed lid for two seconds (count "one thousand one, one thousand two"), and if you can't leave it there for that long, the cooker is too hot. You should also be able to hear just an *occasional* hiss of fat dripping onto the coals and see either heat waves alone or just a wisp of smoke coming out of the stack. Heavy smoke or a continuous "frying" sound from the grill are sure signs that the cooker is too hot. To cool things down, close the ventilation doors tightly for a few minutes.

The biggest challenge in the entire cooking process comes after five-and-a-half to six hours, when it's time for the pig to be turned meat side up. The pig essentially will be done by this time, and the difficulty arises in getting the meat turned without having it fall apart. If you have a second grate, place it upside down on top of the pig so that the wire side is resting against the skin and the pig is "sandwiched" between the two grates. Then, place one person at each of the four corners. Have the people at the corners squeeze the two grates together and quickly turn the pig over so that it is resting skin side down, then remove the extra grate. If you have no second grate, and the pig is in one piece, have four people—wearing gloves—each grasp a ham or a shoulder. When you give the signal, have them lift the pig and roll it toward the front edge of the cooker, allowing the bottom half to fold beneath the top half. Then slide the "folded" pig toward the center and unfold it so that it once again lies flat on the grate, with the meat side facing up. If you had your pig cut in half lengthwise, you should have no trouble turning the two halves; although you'll need to transfer them to opposite sides of the grill so they'll be laid out properly, with the two halves of the split backbone aligned side by side.

Turning the pig is an occasion for much anxious anticipation, and cheers inevitably break out when the meat side first comes into view and turns out to have been cooked to a perfect shade of reddish brown, with no charred spots. However, if you let your coals get too hot so that your first effort results in the meat being a little too dark, take comfort in the fact that the charred areas can easily be pulled or scraped off—and resolve to back off on the heat the next time.

Once the pig is turned, the work is basi-

NORTH CAROLINA BARBECUE : *Flavored by Time*

cally done, and only a few minor tasks remain. First, light a final five-to-ten pounds of charcoal in the second grill. While you're waiting for the briquettes to get ready, generously brush the entire surface of the meat with melted margarine (or simply squirt it from a squeeze bottle) to help glaze and soften the meat. Next, baste the meat thoroughly with your favorite barbecue sauce, allowing the sauce to reach a depth of one inch in the rib cavities. There are people who prefer to use some type of mop to apply the sauce, others shake it out of a bottle onto the pig, and still others use a spoon or a ladle to dip the sauce onto the meat; as far as I can tell, one method is as good as another. Once the last pile of coals is covered with gray ash, scatter them in an even layer across the entire floor of the cooker, as was done with the first batch of briquettes. This final layer of charcoal makes the pig's skin brown and crisp; it also finishes cooking the meat and keeps it hot until it's time for dinner to be served.

It's perfectly acceptable for the cooking crew and the first few guests to stand around the cooker and "pick the pig," pulling off the choicest morsels and dipping them in sauce before popping them into their mouths. If your party is an all-male gathering, it's probably acceptable to simply lay out a few knives and large kitchen forks and let guests help themselves to the roasted pork. However, if women and children are present, you'll need to arrange for one or two persons to help serve meat to the guests. At most eastern North Carolina pig pickings, at least a portion of the pork is removed from the grill and, with the fat and skin removed, chopped to the desired consistency with a heavy cleaver, then seasoned to taste with barbecue sauce. As guests file past the grill with their plates, they have a choice of pulling their own serving of meat from the pig, being helped to slices or chunks of meat by a server, or being served a portion of chopped, seasoned barbecue.

Many cooks, even in the coastal plain, use a basic hot vinegar sauce to season the chopped barbecue, while serving more of a piedmont-style sauce—hot vinegar plus tomato and sweetener—for ladling over the meat that's "picked" from the pig. Your own preferences are all that matter here; I've included several sauce recipes later in the recipe section of this chapter.

Side dishes that are particularly well received at a pig picking include coleslaw, hush puppies or baked corn bread, boiled (barbecued) potatoes, Brunswick stew, and either banana pudding or fruit cobbler for dessert. Recipes for all of these dishes are included in the recipe section. If you want to concentrate your efforts on cooking the pig itself and minimize additional food preparation, you may decide to simply ask each guest to bring a side dish, a beverage, or a dessert.

In eastern North Carolina, Brunswick stew is traditionally cooked over an open fire.

Courtesy N.C. Division of Archives and History

NORTH CAROLINA BARBECUE : *Flavored by Time*

Barbecue Sauces

North Carolina is practically afloat in barbecue sauce. Even if you've never tried mixing up your own sauce, and decide to try one of the recipes listed here, you won't be able to resist adding your own ingredients—which is exactly why there are so many sauces out there. Most importantly, have fun.

Quick-and-Easy Basting and Pig Picking Sauce

  1 gallon apple-cider vinegar
  1 bottle Kraft regular barbecue sauce
  1½ ounces (approximately)
    crushed red pepper
  1 3-ounce bottle Texas Pete hot sauce
  1 tablespoon salt
  1 cup brown or white sugar
  1 stick butter or margarine (optional)

Combine all ingredients in large pot. Bring to a simmer over medium heat and stir until sugar melts. Use to baste pig. After basting, pour into small containers to serve with cooked pig. Refrigerate unused sauce.

Basic Eastern North Carolina Sauce
Courtesy North Carolina Pork Producers Association

  2 quarts apple-cider vinegar
  1½ to 2 ounces crushed red pepper
  2 tablespoons salt, or to taste
  1 tablespoon black pepper, or to taste

Mix all ingredients well. Use to baste pig and to season chopped barbecue to taste. May be stored in tightly sealed container without refrigeration.

Lexington-Style "Dip"

There are a thousand variations of this type sauce. You can follow the basic proportions shown here then bring your own creativity into play.

  3 cups apple-cider vinegar
  ²/₃ cup brown or white sugar
  ¹/₂ cup catsup
  2 tablespoons Texas Pete hot sauce
  1 teaspoon salt
  1 teaspoon black pepper
  1 teaspoon Worcestershire sauce
  1 teaspoon onion powder
  2 teaspoons Kitchen Bouquet browning
    sauce

Combine all ingredients in large pot. Bring to a simmer over medium heat and stir until sugar melts. Let sit for several hours before serving over chopped or sliced pork shoulder. May be stored in tightly sealed container without refrigeration.

Side Dishes for a Barbecue or Pig Picking

Eastern North Carolina Coleslaw

This is my wife Ruthie's recipe, and it's typical of the coleslaw that's served at pig pickings and fish fries along the Roanoke River in Halifax and Martin Counties.

1 medium-size, firm head of cabbage
1 1/2 cups mayonnaise
1/3 cup mustard
3/4 cup sweet pickle cubes
2 tablespoons apple–cider vinegar
1/2 cup sugar
1 tablespoon celery seed
1 1/2 teaspoons salt
1/8 teaspoon black pepper

Keep cabbage refrigerated until ready to use, and do not allow it to reach room temperature once you begin. Remove outer leaves and core from cabbage. Cut head in half and grate fine, using food

processor or hand grater. In large bowl, combine cabbage, mayonnaise, mustard, sweet pickle cubes, vinegar, sugar, and seasonings. Mix thoroughly and chill for one hour before serving. Makes 20 servings.

Piedmont-Style Coleslaw

Here's a tangy, red, piedmont-style coleslaw, similar to what you'll be served at Stamey's in Greensboro or Fuzzy's in Madison. This has a bite to it!

1 medium-size, firm head of cabbage
1/2 cup apple–cider vinegar
1/2 cup sugar
2/3 cup catsup
2 teaspoons salt
2 teaspoons black pepper
2 teaspoons Texas Pete hot sauce

Keep cabbage refrigerated until ready to use. Remove outer leaves and core from cabbage. Cut head in half and grate coarsely, using food processor or hand grater, so that cabbage bits are about the size of BBs. Return cabbage to refrigerator. In small mixing bowl, combine vinegar, sugar, catsup, and seasonings. Mix until well blended. Remove cabbage from refrigerator and pour mixture over it. Mix with large spoon until well blended. (Note: This may look dry at first, but there's plenty of liquid to moisten the cabbage thoroughly if you'll

keep mixing.) *Refrigerate 1 hour before serving.*
Makes 20 servings.

Tad's Barbecue Potatoes

My brother-in-law Tad Everett's recipe is a slight variation on the boiled potatoes found in most eastern North Carolina barbecue restaurants, but the folks around Palmyra, Hobgood, and Oak City always go for these in a big way!

5 pounds potatoes
4 large yellow onions
$^1/_4$ cup bacon drippings
1 20-ounce bottle catsup
$^1/_4$ to $^1/_2$ cup Texas Pete hot sauce, according to taste
$^1/_3$ cup sugar
salt and pepper to taste

Peel potatoes and onions and cut into large chunks. Place in large pot and cover with water. Add remaining ingredients, stir to blend, and bring potatoes to boil. Reduce heat and simmer until potatoes are soft, approximately 30 to 40 minutes. Let potatoes sit over very low heat, stirring occasionally, until ready to serve. Serves 15 hungry men or 10 couples.

Hush Puppies

There are several good hush-puppy mixes on the market, but this is a recipe from scratch that I developed. My friends tell me these pups are as good as any they've ever tasted.

3 cups self-rising white cornmeal
1 cup all-purpose flour
1 tablespoon sugar
1 teaspoon baking powder
1 teaspoon onion powder or 1 medium onion, chopped fine (optional)
2¼ cups buttermilk
2 tablespoons bacon drippings

Combine all dry ingredients. Add buttermilk and bacon drippings and stir mixture until well blended. Pour approximately 4 inches of cooking oil into saucepan or deep fryer and heat to 350 degrees. (For best results, use thermometer to insure that oil doesn't get too hot.) Spread batter evenly, ½-inch thick, on flat surface of pancake turner, using a sharp knife to trim excess from sides and end of turner. With the knife, push ½-inch-wide "fingers" of batter sideways off end of turner and into hot oil, cooking only a few at a time. (You'll need to keep "reloading" the end of the pancake turner with batter, rather than working your way all the way down to the handle.) As hush puppies float, turn them so they brown evenly. Drain on paper towels. Makes about 3 dozen.

Skillet Corn Bread

Some people prefer baked corn bread rather than hush puppies with their barbecue. Here's an easy recipe that produces a tasty, flat corn bread with a crispy crust and top.

1½ cups self-rising cornmeal
½ teaspoon salt
1¼ cups whole milk
2 tablespoons bacon drippings

Preheat oven to 500 degrees. Place bacon drippings in well-seasoned cast-iron skillet. Place skillet in oven for 3 to 4 minutes. While skillet is heating, combine cornmeal, salt, and milk in bowl and stir until well blended. When drippings in skillet are very hot, remove the skillet (using a thick oven mitt) and pour the drippings into the batter, quickly stirring to blend. Quickly pour the batter back into the skillet (it should sizzle) and place it in the oven. Immediately reduce heat to 450 degrees. Bake approximately 20 minutes, or until golden brown. To serve, cut into 6-8 wedge-shaped pieces.

Brunswick Stew

Many residents of rural eastern Carolina pride themselves on their Brunswick stew recipes, and getting together on a winter weekend to "cook a stew" in a large, iron washpot is an activity that, like a pig picking, usually involves several families and consumes an entire Saturday. Most recipes are for 70 to 80 quarts of stew, which are typically divided among the participating families and frozen. (Many churches and organizations also make and sell large quantities of Brunswick stew to raise funds.)

The following recipe is a little more manageable, and makes around 7 quarts. It's very similar to the wonderful Brunswick stew sold at Scotland Neck's Whitaker's Barbecue, which is open only on weekends and is more commonly known simply as "the barbecue stand." You'll notice that this stew does not contain green beans, garden peas, carrots, okra, or other extraneous vegetables commonly added to stews in piedmont North Carolina.

Even though this recipe is designed to be made in a kitchen, rather than over a fire in the backyard, the work will be lighter and you'll have more fun if you invite a friend over for the day to help you make it.

7 pounds chicken
4 28-ounce cans whole tomatoes
3 15-ounce cans baby lima beans
6 cups frozen baby lima beans
6 medium potatoes
2 large yellow onions

4 15-ounce cans cream-style corn

2 cups sugar

3 tablespoons salt, or to taste

1 tablespoon black pepper

1 stick butter or margarine

1½ ounce Texas Pete hot sauce

Wash chicken and cut up, if necessary. (I use leg quarters because they're less expensive, but you may want to use whole chicken in order to get some white meat mixed in.) Place chicken in large pot, barely cover with water, and bring to a boil. Reduce heat and simmer chicken until tender, approximately 40 minutes. Remove chicken from pot and set aside to cool, reserving stock.

Open whole tomatoes and place in second large pot. Use hands to crush tomatoes. Open cans of baby lima beans and add lima bean liquid to tomatoes. Pour baby lima beans from cans into mixing bowl and use hands or potato masher to mash them. Set mashed lima beans aside.

Add six cups of the chicken stock to tomato mixture. Bring mixture to a boil. Reduce heat to medium-high and cook for approximately 40 minutes, or until liquid is reduced by about ¹/₃, stirring frequently.

While liquid is cooking down, bone chicken and shred the chicken meat using a cleaver or food processor. Peel and finely dice potatoes and onions. When liquid is sufficiently reduced, add chicken, mashed lima beans, frozen lima beans, potatoes, and onions. Do not add salt at this point, since it tends to prevent the lima beans from getting soft.

Simmer mixture over very low heat, stirring frequently, for approximately 3½ hours.

Add cream-style corn, sugar, salt, pepper, butter or margarine, and Texas Pete hot sauce. Continue cooking over very low heat for 1 more hour. Because of the sugar you've added (and the sugar in the cream-style corn), the stew is very prone to sticking at this point and will need to be stirred almost constantly until done. Makes approximately 30 servings.

Desserts

Banana Pudding

Banana pudding is the most widely served dessert in North Carolina's barbecue restaurants, probably because it's relatively quick and easy to make, and because the creamy taste and soft texture provide a pleasant contrast to the tangy bite of the barbecue and/or coleslaw. Even though most restaurants make a simpler version, using instant vanilla pudding instead of real custard, the extra trouble required to follow my wife Ruthie's two recipes will be amply rewarded when you serve them to your guests.

I've included a winter version, with a rich, golden meringue topping, and a refrigerated summer version, crowned by whipped cream.

Winter Banana Pudding

7 medium to large bananas, firm and ripe
7 eggs
¾ cup sugar
¼ teaspoon salt
4 cups whole milk
1½ teaspoon vanilla
1 box Nabisco Nilla Wafers

Custard:

Separate yolks and whites of 4 eggs. Put whites aside in large bowl. Slightly beat 4 egg yolks and 3 whole eggs in top of double boiler. Add ½ cup of the sugar and the salt to eggs. Mix well. Scald milk by barely bringing it to a boil in a saucepan. Very slowly stir scalded milk into eggs and sugar. Cook slowly over hot (not boiling) water, stirring constantly until the custard thickens, approximately 20 minutes. (It's okay if it curdles slightly.) Remove from heat, add vanilla, and set aside to cool.

Meringue:

Beat egg whites until soft peaks form. Slowly add ¼ cup sugar and beat until stiff peaks form.

Preheat oven to 425 degrees. Line bottom and sides of a 9- by 13-inch baking dish with Nilla Wafers. Cover wafers with layer of sliced bananas. Spread ¹/3 of custard over bananas. Add another layer of wafers, bananas, and custard. (You will have some custard left over.) Spread top with meringue, making sure that the meringue is touching the side of the dish all the way around (this will prevent shrinking). Bake for 5 minutes or until meringue is browned. Let pudding rest at room temperature for several hours before serving to allow custard to soften and blend with vanilla wafers. Serves 10.

Summer Banana Pudding

7 medium to large bananas, firm and ripe
6 eggs
1¼ cup sugar
¼ teaspoon salt
4 cups whole milk
1½ teaspoon vanilla
1 box Nabisco Nilla Wafers
1 pint whipping cream

Custard:

Slightly beat eggs and place them in top of double boiler. Add ¾ cup sugar and salt. Scald milk by barely bringing it to a boil in a saucepan. Very slowly stir scalded milk into eggs and sugar. Cook slowly over hot (not boiling) water, stirring constantly until custard thickens, approximately 20 minutes. (It's okay if it curdles slightly.) Remove from heat, add vanilla, and set aside to cool. In mixing bowl, beat cream at high speed with electric mixer until it begins to thicken. Continue beating and slowly add ½ cup sugar until cream holds a soft peak. Set aside.

Line bottom and sides of a 9- by 13-inch dish with Nilla Wafers. Cover wafers with layer of sliced bananas. Spread $^1/_3$ of custard over bananas. Spread $^1/_2$ the whipped cream over custard. Add another layer of vanilla wafers, bananas, custard, and whipped cream. (You will have some custard left over.) Refrigerate for several hours before serving to allow custard to soften and blend with vanilla wafers. Serves 10.

Peach Cobbler

Next to banana pudding, peach cobbler is the dessert that seems to have the greatest affinity for barbecue. Keith and Charles Stamey of Stamey's in Greensboro prepare three outstanding fruit cobblers; apple, peach, and cherry; but they say peach outsells apple and cherry by about ten to one. All are usually served topped with vanilla ice cream. They were understandably reluctant to share their recipe, which uses canned peaches, but Ruthie Garner's version, with either frozen or fresh fruit, is also a triumphant finale for a pig picking . . . or any other meal.

Bottom Crust:

2 cups flour

1 teaspoon salt

$^2/_3$ cup butter, cut in ½-inch slices

$^1/_3$ cup ice water

Top Crust:

1 cup flour

$^1/_2$ teaspoon salt

$^1/_3$ cup butter, cut in $^1/_2$-inch slices

2$^1/_2$ teaspoons ice water

Filling:

2$^1/_2$ 20-ounce bags of frozen, unsweetened peaches (or 7 cups of fresh, sliced peaches)

$^1/_3$ cup butter, cut in ½-inch slices

2 cups sugar

4 tablespoons flour

Prepare bottom and top crusts, separately, as follows:

Sift flour and place in food processor with salt and butter. Turning the food processor on in quick bursts, cut butter into flour until mixture is in even bits about the size of small peas. (This can also be done by hand with two knives, a pastry fork, or even your fingers.) Gradually add ice water and continue "pulsing" until mixture begins forming into a ball. (Again, you can work ice water into pastry with a fork or your fingers.) Remove ball of pastry, wrap in plastic, and chill in freezer for 5 minutes.

Roll out pastry for bottom crust and line 9- by 13-inch baking dish. Fill bottom of crust with ½ the peaches. Sprinkle 1 cup sugar and 2 tablespoons flour on top of peaches. Add another layer with the remainder of the peaches, sugar, and flour. Dot top layer with slices of butter.

Roll out top crust and place over peaches, or cut pastry into strips to form lattice crust. Moisten edges of bottom and top crusts with water and use fork to press edges together. Bake at 325 degrees for approximately 1 hour and 45 minutes, or until crust is golden brown. Allow to cool at room temperature for several hours before serving so that any excess juice can be absorbed by pastry. Serves 10.

I know that several of these recipes probably look a little intimidating or complicated for our hurry-up age, but let me remind you that these are meant to be leisure-day dishes, prepared for the pure fun of it, or perhaps as a way of quietly paying tribute to a less-hectic time in our past. These are dishes that have delighted the palates of Tar Heels for generations, and to me, learning to prepare them has been a lot like learning to cook barbecue—a satisfying way of participating in our collective experience as North Carolinians.

North Carolina Barbecue Restaurants

■■■■ What follows is a collection of observations about the barbecue restaurants in North Carolina that, to me, seemed the best, most interesting, or most significant. I want to make it clear that I'm not trying to position myself as a restaurant reviewer or barbecue know-it-all, and I've no doubt left out some spots that deserve to be included. As I've said before, barbecue is a subject that is not only infinitely subjective but is often emotionally charged, and your opinion as to who serves the "best" barbecue is every bit as good as mine. In quite a few cases, historical factors or plain human interest played a major part in my decision to include a particular place. Every writer searches for good stories to tell.

After I began doing barbecue segments for UNC-TV's *North Carolina Now*, I started to receive a lot of phone calls and letters recommending certain places. But I also did a lot of asking around and eavesdropping, as well as quietly stopping into places that I had seen or heard about, usually without identifying myself until I had determined whether it was a place that seemed to warrant further exploration.

Some places didn't want to be included. At

the A & M Grill in Mebane, I had to convince the proprietor that I wasn't trying to sell her something. When I finally managed to overcome that suspicion, she countered with, "Well, we just don't really want to be bothered with talking to anyone," leaving me not only speechless but beaten, as well. (This place serves excellent, wood-cooked barbecue, but don't you dare tell anyone that you heard it from me.) At another spot, which I did include, a son who's taking over the restaurant from his mother was, for whatever reason, consistently rude and oafish as I tried to gather information. It seemed a shame to ignore his mother's friendliness and his parents' fifty years of hard work building a good reputation for their business, so I resisted the temptation to drop all mention of the place.

Mostly, though, the operators of barbecue restaurants—and their offspring—are as nice, patient, and courteous a group as any on the planet. And if I've left out your favorite barbecue spot, what's really important is that you make an effort to let them know how much *you* appreciate them.

Bubba's Barbecue
Hatteras Island

Somehow, I knew in my heart that I couldn't cross North Carolina from one end to the other without encountering a barbecue place named Bubba's. Sure enough, when I got to Hatteras Island at the end of the state, as far east as you can go, there it was. What's more, when I found out that Larry Schauer (Bubba) and his wife Julie (Mrs. Bubba) were pit-cooking barbecue over hickory coals way out here on the virtually woodless Outer Banks, I was, to say the least, intrigued.

I may as well deal right up front with the fact that, despite the nickname, "Bubba" is not really a good ol' boy, at least not in the usual sense, and that the Schauers are . . . well . . . carpetbaggers. He's a native of Minnesota, her family comes from Boston, and they were living on a large farm in West Virginia when they got the idea of pulling up stakes and moving to the Outer Banks, a place they had gown fond of during vacations. The couple's two daughters were getting ready to leave home for college, and Larry and Julie knew the girls wouldn't be coming back home to farm, so when the Schauers saw a house and some land on Hatteras advertised

76

NORTH CAROLINA BARBECUE : *Flavored by Time*

for sale, they decided to buy it. Only after they had sold the farm and moved to Cape Hatteras did they seriously start thinking, "OK . . . now what?"

Larry and Julie had entertained friends with pig pickings on their West Virginia farm, so the "what" turned out to be barbecue. Larry arranged to have hickory wood trucked in from Chesapeake, Virginia. He then built a kitchen with a big, open pit that's visible through plate-glass windows from the U-shaped dining room and started cooking. Since then, as volume has grown, he's added two more wood-fired pits out back. Now, Bubba basically uses the inside pit to get customers salivating as he finishes smoking the meat that's been brought in from outside. Since the inside pit is equipped with an enormous hood that vents the smoke outside, Bubba also conducts merciless atmospheric attacks against the occupants of a campground near the restaurant, loosing billows of tantalizing, aromatic smoke over the helpless campers just before lunch and dinner time. "I really like to get the motorcycle riders, too," he chortles. "They come blasting past here, then about forty yards down the road, they get one whiff and start standing on the brakes."

Bubba and the missus pit-cook pork hams, which they serve either hand-chopped, or sliced thin and piled high on a regular- or large-size sesame-seeded bun. Their sauce, which is vinegar-based, is more like a piedmont-style dip than a strictly down-east mixture. But then, the Outer Banks, with residents and tourists from all over the country, are now "down-east" only in a geographic sense anyway. To accommodate northern and western tastes, Bubba's also offers sandwiches made from sliced, smoked sirloin and thin-sliced, pit-cooked turkey breast. Their menu recommends coleslaw, which is a sweet, mayonnaise-based version, as a topping for all the sandwiches.

Bubba's also offers pork spareribs and chicken, pit-cooked over hickory coals. These entrées can be ordered by themselves (whole, half, or quarter chickens, and whole, half, or quarter slabs of ribs) or on a platter with slaw, fries, potato salad or baked beans, and corn bread. The baked beans are an adaptation of a recipe from Julie's family in Boston, while the baked corn bread (no hush puppies) is a version originally made by Bubba's grandmother, who was a cook in lumber camps along the United States–Canadian border in the early 1900s.

This place is also known up and down the Outer Banks for Mrs. Bubba's homemade pies and cakes—especially the chocolate pie—and for Bubba's bread pudding, which is served with lemon sauce and whipped cream.

There's no question that Bubba's falls outside the parameters of what I would call a traditional North Carolina barbecue place, but his wood-cooked, hand-chopped pork is the real thing—and the beach is a great place for a vacation from tradition.

Bubba's now has two locations: the original, located on N.C. 12 in Frisco, six miles south of the Cape Hatteras Lighthouse, and Bubba's Too, in Avon next to Food Lion. Open daily.

B's Barbecue
Greenville

You won't be able to visit B's without having three images indelibly imprinted on your memory.

The first will be the cars and trucks jamming the dusty, unpaved parking lot and spilling out along the sides of both N.C. 43 and B's Barbecue Road, which form a T-intersection right beside the restaurant. There are no neatly lined parking spaces in B's parking lot, and customers in a hurry constantly pull in and out, leaving their vehicles sitting any-which-way while they dash over to the takeout window. That throws the rest of the parking lot into chaos as well, so a lot of customers simply choose to park on the shoulder of the highway, on the theory that they'll only be exposed to sideswiping from one direction, rather than all four. The amazing thing is that Greenville or Pitt County officials haven't complained about the cars and trucks lining the shoulders, but as co-owner Peggy McLawhorn sweetly explains, "They all like to eat here too." (The fact that the secondary road beside B's is named for the restaurant also tells you a little something.)

The second mental image will be the high proportion of well-dressed, professional men and women among the clientele, either standing in the line that snakes out the front door of this former country store, or waiting their turn for the takeout window in a single file, which on a nice day, forms between picnic tables full of al fresco diners. Oh, there are plenty of working folks, too, in coveralls, jeans, plaid shirts, and boots, but B's is located just a mile north of the large East Carolina-Pitt County regional medical complex, and a lot of the doctors and other health professionals who would warn *you* about the risks of eating too much barbecue regularly slip away to B's on the sly.

The third picture you'll take away from B's is of four of the hardest-working women in eastern North Carolina. Peggy McLawhorn and her three daughters—Tammy, Donna, and Judy—now run B's. On any given day, you'll find at least three of these four women behind the cafeteria-style counter, dressed in baseball caps and T-shirts, cheerfully frazzled and dishing up barbecue and chicken dinners like women possessed. The frantic

NORTH CAROLINA BARBECUE : *Flavored by Time*

B's Barbecue, Greenville

energy of the restaurant was on display when I first visited the place to tape a segment for UNC-TV's *North Carolina Now*. Since B's has no telephone, I was unable to make the usual advance arrangements. When I showed up unannounced with a television crew, Peggy and her daughters were so busy serving the usual lunchtime mob that they hardly noticed my cameraman, Jerome Moore, moving around the kitchen area, practically underfoot, to get the shots he needed. After the crowd thinned a bit, the crew set up lights around one of the booths, and we taped a long sequence of shots of me eating and commenting on B's delicious chopped-pork barbecue and barbecued chicken. Only when

we had finished shooting the entire segment and were packing up the equipment around 2:00 P.M. did Peggy have a chance to get out from behind the counter long enough to come over and ask, "Who *are* you guys, anyway?"

The overwhelming success of B's is sort of a happy accident for the McLawhorn family. Eighteen years ago, Bill and Peggy McLawhorn decided to get out of farming and look for another line of work. Bill had barbecued pigs and chickens more or less as a hobby for years, and he thought he had a pretty good sauce recipe, so the couple decided to look into the barbecue business. "There wasn't any kind of restaurant out on

43," Peggy remembers, "so we bought this old country store and fixed it up the best we could." A brother-in-law named Bob was a partner originally, and since the letter *B* could stand for both Bill and Bob, the restaurant simply became "B's." The McLawhorns built a screened shed behind the restaurant and installed open pits. Today, the smoke from the roasting pork and chicken billows in waves through the screens and across the yard, where it settles over the customers busily eating at the red-painted picnic tables, infusing their clothing with a faint, delightful aroma that reminds them for the rest of the afternoon of the great meal they enjoyed.

B's could probably double its volume if the McLawhorn women could find time to expand, but right now, they're just trying to keep their heads above water in dealing with the current trade. "We sure never thought this business would turn out anything like it has," reflects Peggy McLawhorn, "and it's probably going to get bigger with all the building that's going on out this way." Indeed, the farmland on this side of Greenville is rapidly being transformed into a suburban landscape, with apartment complexes, condominiums, and large new homes crowding out the tobacco barns that have characterized the region for decades.

Bob is no longer involved in the business, and Bill McLawhorn has been in poor health in recent years, so Peggy and the couple's three daughters have assumed the management of the restaurant. Other changes have also occurred. The man who had presided over the pits since the restaurant opened died recently, but another cook who's been with the McLawhorns for several years has stepped in to fill his shoes, and customers swear there's no way the food could get any better than it is at this moment.

B's serves tender, hand-chopped pork barbecue from whole hogs, which are pit cooked over hardwood charcoal. The barbecue is woodsy-flavored from the charcoal but only lightly seasoned, so you'll probably want to add a splash of the restaurant's vinegar-and-pepper sauce for a little extra interest. B's doesn't waste a lot of time, attention, or money on frills, so the sauce on your table will probably have been bottled in any kind of container the McLawhorns could get their hands on. On my several visits, quite a few of the tables were outfitted with Canadian Club whiskey decanters filled with the light red sauce, although I couldn't detect whether Canadian Club was actually one of the ingredients.

Since B's cooks whole hogs, rather than shoulders, ribs are available, but they aren't sold in individual orders. Instead, you'll have to buy a whole set—all the ribs from an entire pig—which is enough to fill a large, four-inch-deep foil pan and costs ten or twelve dollars. These are unbasted, unsauced, slow-

NORTH CAROLINA BARBECUE : *Flavored by Time*

cooked ribs, with slabs of tender meat still attached, and they are, quite simply, out of this world.

B's is as famous for its barbecued chicken as it is for its pork barbecue. The half-chickens grill for hours over a low charcoal fire and are immersed, just before they're served, in a vinegar-based sauce similar to the one designed for the chopped pig. The chicken is not overcooked so that it's sliding off the bones, and the vinegar flavor is not overwhelming, as it is in many versions of eastern-style barbecued chicken. Even after the chicken is soaked briefly in the sauce, the skin remains crisp, and the meat has just the right firmness and texture. You won't find better grilled chicken inside the borders of North Carolina (and perhaps, not anywhere else, either).

The side dishes at B's are traditional but not extensive. In addition to the standard coleslaw, B's serves eastern North Carolina boiled potatoes and home-style green beans, so that it's possible to put together a chicken dinner that's a relatively healthy, low-fat meal. Hush puppies have been replaced here by squares of traditional, flat-as-a-pancake, baked corn bread, which is a delicious and refreshing change of pace.

The chicken, pork barbecue, and side dishes at B's are all good enough to put the restaurant at or near the top of the list of the state's very best barbecue spots.

B's is located north of Greenville (toward Rocky Mount) on N.C. 43, one mile north of the medical center. If you're coming into Greenville from Wilson on U.S. 264, turn left at the first stoplight onto B's Barbecue Road and travel 1.2 miles to the intersection with N.C. 43; you'll find B's on the right of this intersection. Closed Sunday and Monday.

The Skylight Inn
Ayden

OK, here's the plan. You live your whole life in this little town of maybe a couple of thousand people. You don't go off to college, and you don't seek an executive position with a fast-track company offering excellent chances for advancement. You just stay right there and work. You open a little place, nothing fancy or even very noticeable, not even on the main highway. You put in day after day of long, inconvenient hours—hot, dirty, greasy, back-hurting, splinter-in-your-finger, eye-stinging, foot-aching work. Do it all again the next day. And the next.

After thirty years, you're famous in your field. You've received dozens of awards. You're praised in national magazines and on network television. Presidents have tried your product and offered their compliments. And people from all over who've heard about you beat a path to this little, unsophisticated town—it calls itself the "Collard Capital of the World," for Pete's sake—just to buy your product. You've even had them tell you they were fixing to transport it halfway around the world, to Turkey or someplace. But there's been no advertising agency, no public relations campaign. Shoot, for years there wasn't even a sign out front. Just word of mouth—that'll do. Now it's, "Oh, Pete, *Southern Living*'s on the phone—can you talk to them?"

Got it? Okay, on three—down, set . . . hut—hut—hut!

Ayden, in Pitt County, some twelve miles south of Greenville, is well known in the region for some state-championship-caliber 1-A football over at Ayden-Grifton High School. But the local team never pulled off a play as big as *that*. Something that unlikely, that American, could only happen in the world of barbecue, where the only thing that matters, ultimately, is the verdict the public renders on your work. No use just to plan it or talk about it. You've got to produce—every day.

Pete Jones (he doesn't use the Walter B.) never wanted to do anything else. "I'd sit in school, as far back as the fifth or sixth grade, and daydream about having my own barbecue place," he remembers. After high school—where acquaintances with stars in

their eyes spent their time daydreaming about little else but getting out of Ayden—he went to work cooking barbecue for his uncle. He did that for awhile, then finally opened a business of his own in 1948. Nearly forty years later, he went out and found someone to build a silver-painted wooden dome, vaguely like the one atop the United States Capitol but smaller, on top of his otherwise undistinguished brick building. *National Geographic* had just identified his place as the barbecue capital of the *world*, and considering all the previous awards, and since the restaurant was a little off the beaten track, he figured he might as well make it easier for people to know that this was it. This was the place. The capital.

Anyone who knows barbecue knows that family and heritage are important. You have to love feeding people . . . love watching them enjoy your food. You also have to be fiercely determined to keep that happy look on their faces, and at least part of that is passed along in the blood. Pete's great-great-grandfather began selling barbecue in Ayden out of the back of a covered wagon around 1830, and while the family barbecue business hasn't run continually all that time, his family has been at it for a great many years. In acknowledgment of how it all began, there's now a covered wagon out front bearing the name of Pete's place, the Skylight Inn. But that's a recent addition, basically for the benefit of

The Skylight Inn, Ayden

tourists, and illustrative of Pete's no-nonsense attitude about what it takes to become successful is the fact that the place didn't have *any* kind of a sign for a long time. As word spread around Ayden, Grifton, Winterville, and Greenville about Pete's barbecue, everyone simply called the place Pete Jones's. And as Pete said pointedly years ago, "A place like this don't need any sign."

Don't come into the Skylight, operated by Pete and his nephew Jeff Jones, expecting any gingham tablecloths or cutesy little pig cutouts. The decor could perhaps best be described as absent. There are no menus and the tables are bare, adorned only with bottles of Texas Pete, pepper vinegar, and toothpicks. There are no waitresses either. If you want to eat at Pete's, you come up to the counter, order, pay, and carry your food back to the table like everybody else, thank you. This is probably the only barbecue place in the known world that doesn't have sweet ice tea—or any ice tea. Everything there is to drink comes in a bottle, the sixteen-ounce, soft-drink variety, and when it comes time for dessert, you might as well not look around for the banana pudding, or the peach cobbler and ice cream. What you do is amble over to the wire display rack in the corner and select a moon pie, a fig cake, or maybe one of those double oatmeal cookies stuck together with cream filling.

But then you don't come to Pete's for dessert. You come for a barbecue sandwich on a bun, topped with yellow coleslaw. (He only recently stopped using plain, white loaf bread—light bread—in favor of hamburger-type buns.) Or you come for a paper tray of chopped barbecue, a square slab of baked corn bread, and a little dish of slaw. That's the way it's served, too: tray of barbecue on the bottom, sheet of restaurant tissue, piece of corn bread sitting on top of that, more tissue, and the paper container of slaw and a plastic fork balanced on top of the stack. That way you can pick the whole thing up in one hand and have the other hand free to carry your drink. When you pay, you notice Pete has no cash register, just a pile of bills and currency on the back counter from which he rapidly makes change. What you *can't* see is that he also keeps a loaded gun beneath the counter, just in case.

When you get back to your table, you survey the three or four items on your table, counting the Pepsi. That's it. There are no french fries, no potato salad, no baked beans, and right smack in the middle of the Collard Capital of the World, no collard greens or other vegetables.

All right, now we're down to the fact that the business end of this enterprise isn't up front in the kitchen or dining room—it's out back. That's where you find a wood lot of oak and hickory big enough to remind you of a small lumberyard, and a small, detached, cinder-block building where tending the fires and cooking is basically Jeff's responsibility. Out of an ordinary open fireplace, Jeff shovels out live coals and scatters them under the whole, split pigs roasting in three-foot-high pits. He works from the top, dropping the coals through the metal bars on which the meat rests, maneuvering the shovel around the sides of the meat. In the gloom of the unlit building, a shaft of white sunlight streaming through an open door reveals dust-like floating particles of fine ash, which, together with the billowing smoke and the scraping of the shovel, make the whole scene look like what we called "the bad place" when I was growing up. (I visited in February; imagine this in August.)

The roasted, falling-apart-tender pigs are transported to the kitchen, where skin and fat are separated from the lean meat. But they aren't separated for too long, because as the meat is sprinkled with Texas Pete and vinegar (no other sauce) and thoroughly chopped, you notice that a fair amount of the fat and skin is itself chopped and mixed back in with the shredded, crunchy, reddish brown outside meat and the white or light brown meat from the shoulders, hams, and loin. Now there are those who would shudder at the fat content of Pete's barbecue, but then those people probably wouldn't be caught dead in any kind of barbecue place to begin with, not even those places up in the piedmont producing a much leaner blend. If we can all agree that eating barbecue is like firing a cholesterol bullet straight into our own hearts, we can simply note that Pete's merely packs a heftier slug. (A little bit of the cooked pig finds its way into his signature baked corn bread, too. The square baking pans get a dollop of liquefied pork fat—euphemistically called "drippings"—before the corn bread batter is ladled in, and when you peer into the oven, you can see the hot grease bubbling merrily up over the edges of the inch-and-a-half-thick corn bread.)

Pete's barbecue is, simply, unlike any other, and certainly different from most eastern barbecue, which tends to be a little drier and have a more pronounced vinegar-pepper tang. Since it's the fat that carries the flavor of the seasoning through barbecue, or most any food, Pete gets more of the wood-smoke taste in his meat than just about any other place I've found in the east, and the texture is moist and luxuriant to the tongue without being over sauced. All in all, it is wonderful but powerful stuff, and probably should carry a disclaimer stamped onto each paper tray— "Warning: can cause drowsiness. Do not eat before driving or operating heavy machinery." My UNC Television cameraman, Jeff Anderson, who's normally a bundle of nervous energy, smacked his lips through a tray of Pete's barbecue, then had no sooner climbed back into the van when he mumbled something about "wanting to lie down," then slept throughout the two-hour return trip to the studio.

The Skylight Inn really is world-famous on the insider barbecue circuit, and although reputations in food-and-drink can be queerly and swiftly made, Pete's has held up long enough to be taken seriously. Whether you end up pronouncing his barbecue the absolute best you've ever tasted, or characterize it as merely an interesting regional oddity, it's very well worth going out of your way to visit the Skylight Inn. Cut way down on your fat intake for a week, then take N.C. 11 south out of Greenville, turn left on West Third Street, then right on Lee Street (old N.C. 11). You won't be able to miss the cars and trucks filling the parking lot and parked along both sides of the road. Closed Sunday.

Ken's Grill
LaGrange

Ken's Grill is an unobtrusive little place, the kind of spot you might blow right past without noticing as you travel on U.S. 70 to Morehead City or Beaufort. Before I had a chance to visit, I had received several phone calls about the barbecue at Ken's over a period of several months. I finally found myself passing through the area on a Wednesday— one of only two days of the week Ken's Grill prepares barbecue, the other being Saturday— so I decided to pick up a sandwich for the road. A half-hour earlier, coincidentally, a traveling companion and I had sampled the barbecue at a well-known restaurant in Kinston. I found that barbecue limp and uninspiring, but we both thought the meat from Ken's was in a totally different class: firm, chunky, tender, and perfectly seasoned, with a delightful, savory aftertaste that lingered pleasantly on the tongue after the sandwich was consumed.

Only after arriving at Ken's with a UNC-TV camera crew, several months later, did I discover that his whole-hog barbecue is not cooked over a wood-fired pit, as I had supposed, but in an electric cooker. Now I can be pretty stubborn about some things, but when presented with incontrovertible evidence by Ken Eason and his brother David that it is possible to produce superior barbecue cooked in a manner other than over hardwood coals, I decided to relax my thinking a bit and go with the flow. Not many people are able to get the results Ken achieves without the wood, but there's no denying that his barbecue is simply delicious, and I'll consider myself fortunate to have some of it whenever I'm in the neighborhood.

The other thing I really liked about Ken Eason's place was this modest, unassuming man's air of flattered surprise at being singled out for recognition. When our camera crew arrived, we found the little restaurant shined up spic-and-span, with both the older women and the fresh-faced teenage girls who work there proudly and identically turned out in neat, matching shorts; white cotton blouses; perky white paper hats; and sharp, obviously new, navy blue aprons. A lot of his regular customers from around LaGrange were on hand, too, and most of them were quick to offer unsolicited testimonials about the con-

sistent quality of the food at Ken's. The restaurant is quite a community gathering place, with the bulk of Eason's business coming from his neighbors. However, during the spring and summer, the grill gets a lot of beach traffic on Fridays and Saturdays, beginning with Easter weekend.

Ken and David Eason have an infectious enthusiasm about their place, which carries on a tradition begun when their father owned and operated "Skin's" Drive-In nearby. The elder Eason began cooking and selling barbecue on Saturdays only, and when Ken took over the operation upon his father's death in 1974, he continued the practice, expanding to Wednesdays after he built the present seventy-seat restaurant in 1980. Ken still uses his father's secret sauce recipe, which is obviously what elevates his barbecue from the ordinary to the realm of the sublime, and several local residents—who aren't exactly in the Sahara when it comes to the availability of fine barbecue—pronounced it the best they've ever eaten. The hand-chopped pork is served in sandwiches and in paper trays, accompanied by mayonnaise-based coleslaw and, as long as they last, a piece or two of crisp, fried pork skin. Hush puppies are available, naturally, and the method of forming them at Ken's is something I hadn't observed before. The cook piles the thick batter on the blade of a long, metal turner as though she's laying mortar; trowels it flat on the top and sides

NORTH CAROLINA BARBECUE : *Flavored by Time*

with a knife; then, in a blur of speed, cuts straight down through the batter, pushing one-half-inch-wide "fingers" of the mixture off the end of the turner and into the hot cooking oil.

Besides barbecue, Ken's offers thick, hand-patted burgers, which are typically served country-style—topped with cheese, coleslaw, and homemade chili. There's also a different special every day, including Fridays, when Ken's serves its own version of the thick fish stew that's probably the number one local delicacy in the area—surpassing even barbecue.

Ken's Grill occupies a small, square building on the south side of U.S. 70 outside LaGrange, roughly halfway between Goldsboro and Kinston. Closed Sunday—and remember, barbecue is served only on Wednesday and Saturday.

Bob Melton's Barbecue
Rocky Mount

Bob Melton's is the oldest real, sit-down barbecue restaurant in North Carolina; it's been nestled on the same shady spot beside the Tar River for more than seventy years. The rambling, white-frame building, so familiar to the generations that remained faithful to the place, is gone now, but a new dining room has been built on its foundations. Inside, the wood floors and light wood paneling of the original eatery have been closely reproduced, so the *feel* of the place is very much as it has always been, and the peaceful view of the river hasn't changed at all. There have been some major changes in the way the barbecue and other dishes are prepared, but a lot of old-timers vow that everything still tastes the same, which may be due largely to both pleasant memories and the management's ability to maintain much of the original atmosphere of this eastern North Carolina institution.

I can clearly remember visiting Melton's in the '50s, when it seemed far outside of town. It was reached by an unpaved road that formed a steep, eroded gully through the woods until it emerged in Melton's dirt parking lot. Wooden steps led up to an unscreened, creaky wooden porch that rambled around two sides of the building, while an old-fashioned screened door provided access to a main dining room that contained long wooden tables and a well-worn board floor. Today, the kitchen and takeout area occupy the old parking lot, while a brand new paved lot has been built on the opposite side of the restaurant. But even with all the changes, the exterior is still white clapboard (well, OK, vinyl siding), and the first view of Melton's new layout provides a comforting feeling of familiarity.

Bob Melton, who died years ago, was the man who probably did more than any other to popularize eastern-style barbecue. Like so many other famous barbecuers, this farmer, merchant, and horse trader got into the barbecue business as a part-time venture. Melton started out with some barbecue pits and a simple shed in 1922, and so many people made their way down to the riverbank to buy his barbecue to take home that he decided to open a sit-down restaurant, which was built in 1924. A wall-mounted menu board from 1929 shows that a plate of barbecue and boiled potatoes cost forty-five cents (forty cents without the potatoes), while a barbecue sandwich was fifteen cents. All soft drinks were a nickel, and a large admonition printed in red across the bottom of the sign warned, "No Whiskey Allowed." However, the premises were still wet from time to time due to the fact that Melton had built his restaurant in the flood plain of the Tar River. But business never really slowed much, even during high water, as customers made their way to Melton's door in boats. (Flood control measures in recent years have largely alleviated this problem.)

For at least ten years, Melton's was the only barbecue restaurant in eastern North Carolina, and even the citizens of Wilson, now a barbecue hotbed, traveled the eighteen miles between the two towns to eat at Melton's. In the early '30s, Adam Scott opened his famous restaurant on the back porch of his home in Goldsboro, eventually leading to quite a rivalry between Rocky Mount and Goldsboro—really between Melton's and Scott's—for bragging rights as to which city produced the best barbecue. In 1958, the year Melton died, Rocky Mount appeared to have gained an edge in this competition when *Life* magazine referred to Melton as "the king of southern barbecue."

Both Bob Melton and Adam Scott built their reputations for cooking whole hogs by laying them out on metal rods over beds of oak and hickory coals. At Melton's, one added innovation was the placement of a layer of sheet tin just above the roasting pigs, so that coals could be shoveled on top as well as underneath—providing heat from both above and below the meat. It's ironic that although both men deplored the practice of preparing barbecue on gas cookers, the present-day managers of both restaurants have now switched to this cooking method for reasons of cost and efficiency. What's more, Melton's has also switched to cooking all pork shoulders, rather than the whole hog. Tommy Smith, the present owner, states unequivocally that he thinks Melton's barbecue is better now than it ever was, and there's no question that the majority of his customers seem to agree that it's at least as good as al-

NORTH CAROLINA BARBECUE : *Flavored by Time*

Bob Melton's provides a restful view of the Tar River.

ways. Apparently most patrons think the tenderness and seasoning of the meat make up for any lack of wood-smoked taste, which can no longer be considered a prime characteristic of eastern-style barbecue. One lady who told me she had eaten at Melton's at least once a week for the past forty-five years said, "It's just the same as it's always been."

Personally, I found the barbecue to be well seasoned and tasty, with quite a peppery personality. Like most whole-hog eastern barbecue, Melton's version tends to run to the dry side, perhaps because it's chopped, by machine, a little too finely for my taste. But then, Rocky Mount barbecue has always been chopped finer than that in other cities, and Melton's has more than enough loyal customers from all over the country to be able to claim that it's producing barbecue exactly to its customers' tastes.

Melton's coleslaw is very yellow, with both dry and prepared mustard added, along with a small amount of mayonnaise. The exceptionally light and crispy hush puppies have a trademark ridge along the top that is apparently due to an idiosyncrasy of their hushpuppy machine. Boiled potatoes are still served, and they're pretty much like those Bob Melton added to a barbecue plate for an extra nickel back in '29, but the Brunswick stew is essentially a canned product and can't be considered authentic. Melton's is notable in that it offers a variety of home-style vegetables, including sweet potatoes, green beans, black-eyed peas, cabbage, and collard greens. The restaurant also sells quite a bit of fried chicken, most of it in barbecue-and-chicken combination plates. The consistently moist and flavorful chicken has a golden, crispy crust. A very tasty version of banana pudding, with lots of vanilla wafers, is available to top off your meal.

The dining room at Melton's is always a clean, cheerful place to eat. There is lots of sunshine streaming through the windows and a great view of the bucolic Tar River, shaded by large trees along its banks. All in all, the restaurant offers a superior dining experience, and even if there are changes, we ought to be thankful that they've at least managed to preserve the *essence* of this barbecue landmark.

Melton's is located on the north side of Rocky Mount, just off U.S. 301 Business, which is also known as Church Street. Turn on Melton Drive and follow the signs to the restaurant. Open daily.

Bill's
Wilson

Bill's isn't a barbecue place—it's an empire.

Some thirty-five years ago, Bill Ellis bought a run-down, country drive-in with a reputation as a less-than-wholesome teenage hangout. Today, in addition to a sprawling, white brick restaurant, Bill's place south of Wilson includes a suite of offices, a garage, and twenty-five or thirty catering trucks of all sizes, including several seventy-five-foot tractor-trailers. All the vehicles are emblazoned with his logo—a bright red silhouette of the state of North Carolina with the words *BILL ELLIS, Wilson, NC* in white and *Barbecue* in blue—and with his slogan: "We doos 'em right!"

Inside the bustling restaurant, which has several dining rooms, the red, white, and blue logo can be seen on T-shirts and hats for sale in the lobby and on dozens of color pictures of NASCAR-type race cars sponsored by Ellis, looking for all the world like really fast barbecue delivery vehicles. Another Ellis passion, softball, is evidenced by scores of trophies and team photographs, with hundreds of uniformed chests bearing his ubiquitous visual trademark.

The Ellis logo looks a bit like a campaign sign, which is not inappropriate considering the thousands of political gatherings and state-government functions he's catered during the past thirty years. In fact, on many occasions, Ellis, his son Marty, and other members of his food-service teams have traveled out of state to cater functions organized by North Carolina's recruiters of new business and industry. Several years ago, the Ellis team took an eighteen-wheeler all the way to Palm Springs, California, for such a function, and Ellis now proudly advertises "coast-to-coast catering."

The size and visibility of the catering business aside, Bill's restaurant offers eastern North Carolina–style barbecue victuals that almost perfectly define this coastal plain cuisine. While his barbecue and side dishes can't really be described as distinguished, they are consistent, and patrons know exactly what to expect each and every time they walk through the door. What Bill's actually serves up is comfort food, and meal hours always find his expansive parking lot jammed with folks who need comforting.

Bill's is the quintessential eastern barbecue, strongly flavored by salt, vinegar, and red pepper, with crushed pepper flakes and seeds readily visible throughout the chopped meat. I discovered, happily, that Bill's does not chop the barbecue superfine, unlike some other prominent eastern establishments; instead, the meat has an attractive shredded texture. There is no wood-smoke taste in this barbecue, since Ellis cooks whole hogs on gas-fired pits.

However, as I've mentioned, an open-pit taste is not a characteristic that many easterners seem to prize any longer in their barbecue. Bill's version contains little fat or gristle, although it is heavily laced with bits of finely chopped skin. Some people swear that good barbecue *must* have skin chopped up in it, others don't like it at all; personal preference is everything here. The pork itself is flavorful and tender, which is partly due to slow cooking at precisely controlled temperatures and partly to the fact that Bill's has its own hog farm where the pigs' diet and other factors can be controlled.

Boiled potatoes are a side dish that almost always accompany Bill's barbecue. While some barbecue cooks around the coastal plain add a fair amount of red pepper and/or tomato sauce to the water in which the potatoes boil, there was little or no evidence of this in Bill's version. The potatoes intentionally seem to be left a bit on the bland side to help balance the acidity of the barbecue, but they're very pleasing, with only a little salt and just a hint of pork drippings or other, similar seasoning.

Bill's coleslaw is minced very fine, with the predominant flavors coming from vinegar, sugar, and mustard; there appears to be little or no mayonnaise. This is both a very sweet and a very tart slaw, with the characteristic eastern North Carolina yellow hue.

Frankly, I was a little disappointed in the Brunswick stew, which I found on the dry side and relatively tasteless. Most people in the coastal plain seem to like sweet Brunswick stew, but Bill's stew had no discernible hint of sugar or other sweetener. In addition to larger-than-optimum lima beans (rather than baby butter beans) and large-kerneled yellow corn, the stew also contained green beans—something you might expect to find in the piedmont but certainly not in the heart of eastern North Carolina barbecue-and-stew country. Maybe they were just having a bad stew day when I visited. Most of the folks who flock to Bill's were raised on Brunswick stew, and it seems unlikely that his restaurant could turn out a consistently marginal version of this dish without word getting around.

Luckily, the shortcomings of the Brunswick stew are more than balanced by the delicious crispness of Bill's cornsticks, which are lighter than other versions I've encountered. The crust is satisfyingly crunchy all the way around, while the center is reminiscent of good, honest, flat-baked corn bread or corn pone, with a straightforward taste of white cornmeal. In addition to the cornsticks, I was served hush puppies, which I found tasty and light, if not particularly crispy.

Bill's is also famous for fried chicken, which is not only a staple of his catered meals but which is also offered in a "barbecue and chicken combination" plate served in the restaurant. I had heard a lot about Bill's chicken, and the large breast I was served more than

lived up to my expectations—the skin was golden and crisp, but not brittle, while the white meat was tender and dotted in places with beads of juice.

A particularly nice touch was the fact that my waitress left an entire pitcher of ice tea to accompany my meal. In keeping with the tastes of the region, the tea is very, very sweet, but it's a well-brewed, clear, and mild beverage.

You might say that Bill's barbecue and fixings occupy the safe, comfortable middle, rather than the exhilarating but precarious edge. You'll find very little, if anything, to criticize among Bill's menu items, which are served promptly and with smile. You'll also enjoy soaking up some of the real eastern North Carolina ambiance of the place, as well as knowing that you've dined with one of the biggest names (or at least the most tirelessly promoted) in North Carolina barbecue.

Bill's is located on the southwest side of Wilson, near Wiggins Mill Reservoir. From U.S. 264, turn south on N.C. 42 and travel approximately one mile. Turn left on Forest Hills Road, travel another mile, and you'll see Bill's on the left, at the intersection with Downing Street. From Interstate 95, head east on N.C. 42 into Wilson. Turn right onto Forest Hills Road and proceed one mile to the restaurant. From U.S. 301, travel south 1.7 miles past the intersection with U.S. 264 (passing Parker's Barbecue on the right), turn

NORTH CAROLINA BARBECUE : *Flavored by Time*

right on Forest Hills Road, and travel one mile; you'll spot Bill's on the right side. Open daily.

Mitchell's Barbecue
Wilson

If family ties are the only bonds strong enough to hold together a successful barbecue business over many years, they're probably also the only influence strong enough to make a newcomer go into the barbecue business in Wilson, North Carolina—the home of Parker's and Bill's, two of the biggest barbecue names in eastern North Carolina. Ed Mitchell not only took on these two barbecue giants, he's earning a reputation for turning out some of the most genuine-tasting barbecue in the region—along with an absolutely wonderful selection of home-style vegetables. Mitchell's is just a little place, so in Wilson, he's definitely a David among Goliaths, but his cozy eatery and takeout counter is a treasure that lovers of real, pit-cooked barbecue will want to seek out.

For many years, Ed's parents, Willie and Doretha Mitchell, ran a mom-and-pop neighborhood grocery store on U.S. 301 (also known as Ward Boulevard), in one of Wilson's predominantly black neighborhoods. The proceeds from that little store went to raise three sons, including Ed, who graduated from Fayetteville State University, served as an army officer in Vietnam, and got a white-collar job with a state government agency.

Willie Mitchell handled most of the responsibilities of running the grocery, and when he died in 1990, Ed's mother was left to take up the reins as best she could. Business began to fall off, and four months after his father's passing, Ed stopped in one day and found Doretha sitting behind the cash register in a visibly depressed state. When Ed asked what was wrong, his mother replied, "I've been sitting here all day, and I've only taken in twelve dollars." In an effort to cheer Doretha, Ed asked what he could prepare for her to eat, and she replied wistfully that she was in a mood for "some good, old-fashioned barbecue . . . not that gas-cooked stuff." Being a dutiful son, Ed got up early the next morning and bought a thirty-four-pound pig, collected a load of wood, and dragged an old cooker out of the garage behind the store. He spent several hours barbecuing the pig, and when it was done, Ed chopped and seasoned the meat, filling a large pan with the barbecue.

Shortly afterwards, Ed and Doretha were enjoying their pit-cooked treat in the store's back room when some customers came in and spied the pan of chopped pork. As they exclaimed over the barbecue's appearance and aroma, Ed gave his mother an enormous wink and stage-whispered, "Mom . . . sell them some!" Acting as though it was the most normal thing in the world, Doretha opened a package of buns and made several barbecue sandwiches for the delighted customers. After they left, it wasn't long before other customers came in asking for the barbecue. Before the day was done, Ed and his mother had not only sold the meat from the entire pig, but also had a new vision for transforming the struggling grocery store into a thriving enterprise.

It took a couple of years before Ed was able to arrange his affairs and quit his job, but he followed through with the dream of going into the barbecue business. Before he began his operation, Ed set out to find someone who had a real, firsthand knowledge of old-fashioned pit-cooking techniques. He finally made the acquaintance of eighty-year-old James Kirby, whom he credits with devising and building a pit setup that doesn't demand as much time and labor as other designs.

Kirby had Ed clean the old garage out back, then set to work building a waist-high brick box, which was partially filled with sand. Then two oil tank–type cookers of the sort normally used at pig pickings (minus the wheels) were sunk horizontally partway into the sand, which serves as insulation around the bottom of the cookers, helping to hold in the heat of the charcoal and hickory-wood coals. The idea behind the setup is to allow Mitchell to put his pigs on the cooker at night and leave them unattended, so they're done when he arrives in the morning. With the sand preventing the heat from dissipating, and with all the vents closed nearly tight, the beds of coals are effectively "banked," and the pits slowly cook to perfection the smaller pigs Mitchell prefers, with no need for the meat to be turned. The first thing the next morning, the meat is chopped and seasoned so that it's ready for the first lunch customer.

Mitchell's still occupies the small, cinder-block building that housed the grocery store, although a recent remodeling has added extra seating space. Even so, there are still probably fewer than a dozen booths and tables. But the place is clean and the atmosphere is cheerful and uplifting, with pictures of Ed's son Ryan, a star football running back at Wilson's Beddingfield High School, adorning the walls. (After all, this place is all about family.) Behind and to the side of the main building, a smaller structure—the former garage—is identified in large painted letters as "The Pit," and a reassuring cloud of smoke can usually be seen billowing out the doors at most times of the day or night. Charcoal is the main source of fuel for the two cookers, and soaked lengths of hardwood are added on top of the charcoal briquettes to produce extra smoke.

To this day, Mitchell gets a little emotional when he thinks about how proud his father would be to see the family business doing well, if in an altered form. Remembering Willie's frequent advice to "keep it simple," he plans to keep the restaurant seating fairly limited, and to focus on both the takeout business and catering. Servicing parties and special events already accounts for some 30 percent of Mitchell's trade, and he hopes one day to derive at least half his income from this end of the business.

Ed, a large, affable man with a gray beard, is the owner of the restaurant, but he says his mother Doretha is still "the driving force" behind Mitchell's. His brothers, Stevie and Aubry, are both involved in the business, as well. Together, this family has put together a menu that's totally different from that found at most barbecue restaurants. For one thing, Mitchell's hand-chopped barbecue—which is lean, moist, and delicious—is complemented by ribs, chicken, and porkchops, all pit-cooked. But the real shining star at this place is the selection of home-style fresh vegetables: well-seasoned collard and mustard greens, cabbage, rutabagas, homemade macaroni-and-cheese, and other selections that vary according to the season. Ed says, "Back in the old days, when you came in from a day of working in tobacco, there was a spread laid out so you knew somebody had been doing some *cookin'* . . . and that's the kind of meal we want to provide here." The array of fresh vegetables is complemented by baked corn bread, meringue-topped banana pudding, and old-

fashioned fried apple and peach turnovers. "We make everything fresh that day," says Ed, "and when we sell out, that's it."

After three years in business, Mitchell still seems a little surprised that the restaurant has generated such a positive response. "I've never owned anything anyone wanted before this," he explains. "Now I'm curious to see what will happen and how far we can go." Coincidentally, the week after I first visited Ed Mitchell's place, a viewer who had seen several of my UNC-TV segments on other barbecue restaurants left a long phone message describing Mitchell's in glowing terms, concluding with the admonition, "You simply *must* add this place to your list."

Mitchell's is located on the west side of U.S. 301 (Ward Boulevard), several blocks north of its intersection with U.S. 264. Open daily.

Parker's
Wilson

U.S. 301 used to be the main north-south artery through eastern North Carolina, the equivalent of today's Interstate 95 for those traveling from the Northeast toward Florida. In 1946, at the beginning of the post–World War II transportation explosion, Parker's opened alongside U.S. 301 as a barbecue-and-fried-chicken restaurant (a motor court was added later). With this fortuitous meeting of time, place, and great food, it isn't surprising that today Parker's is one of the best-known names in eastern North Carolina dining. Even though I-95, which roughly parallels U.S. 301, passes some seven miles to the west, plenty of travelers still detour off the interstate to eat at the restaurant, which advertised itself for years as "North Carolina's Famous Eating Place."

However, the tobacco markets in Wilson were just as important as the transportation explosion in helping to build Parker's reputation. In North Carolina's flue-cured-tobacco belt, barbecue has always been associated with celebrating the harvesting and curing of the yearly crop of the golden leaf. Farmers would not only organize barbecues for those who had helped them pick and "put in" their crop, but would often celebrate the sale of their tobacco at one of the warehouse auctions by joining friends and family for a barbecue meal at a place like Parker's. A large photographic mural of workers outside a tobacco barn hangs on one wall at Parker's, acknowledging the importance of the tobacco culture to the restaurant's success, and the crop can still be found growing within a stone's throw of Parker's barbecue pits.

Brothers Graham and Ralph Parker, and a cousin, Henry Parker Brewer, founded Parker's, building the restaurant with timber that had been floated up the Tar River from the family farm in Pitt County. Current co-owner Bobby Woodard, who's been with the restaurant for nearly forty of its fifty years, says it took about ten years for the place to become established. The turning point occurred when Ralston Purina opened a large feed plant in the area in 1955 and contracted Parker's to feed over seventeen thousand people at the grand opening—for seventy-five cents each. The day of the big feed, which took place at the county fairgrounds, was the only day in its fifty-year history that Parker's has ever been closed for business.

Henry Brewer died in 1987, the same year that Graham and Ralph decided to retire and sell the original Wilson restaurant to Woodard and Don Williams, another longtime employee. (Another Parker's location in Greenville is owned by a brother and nephew of Graham and Ralph, but it is run as an entirely separate business.)

A meal at Parker's is all about custom and continuity, rather than adventure. Most people know exactly what they'll order even before they arrive: chopped barbecue, fried chicken, coleslaw, boiled potatoes, Brunswick stew, corn sticks, and ice tea. Unless you're planning on spending the afternoon sawing logs or chopping cotton, this is a repast that will almost certainly put you out of commission for the rest of the day if it's consumed at noon. But then, I've noticed that a great many of Parker's customers have attained an age and level of wisdom at which a dignified afternoon nap would not be considered out of the ordinary. Many of these customers have been dining regularly at Parker's for forty years or more, and their meals there seem like quiet observances of the changing of the seasons and the orderly passage of the years: a rite celebrating the slow, ceaseless rhythms of life on the flat, sandy coastal plain.

Like all the similar restaurants of its era, Parker's used to pit cook its barbecue over oak coals. In recent years, the Wilson restaurant has been mildly criticized for supposedly cooking its pigs with gas. This criticism is not entirely accurate, and is partly due to some confusion about the cooking practices between the two different Parker's locations. It's true that gas hoods have been installed over the regular pits at the Wilson restaurant, but they're used only at the end of the cooking process—basically just to brown and crisp the skin. During most of the eight to ten hours that the whole hogs are on the pits, they're roasting over hardwood charcoal, which, in my opinion, is virtually indistinguishable from oak or hickory coals in terms of the taste it adds to the barbecue. Hardwood charcoal is also used by a couple of other outstanding eastern restaurants: Stephenson's in rural Johnston County, near Raleigh, and B's in Greenville. The gas burners at Parker's allow the pigs to crisp up and finish cooking without having to be turned

skin-side down for the final couple of hours. In my judgment, that's a fair compromise between tradition and labor-saving technology.

Like its crosstown competition, Bill's Barbecue, Parker's has been raising its own hogs since the 1970s. The tenderness and flavor of pork has much to do with a hog's diet and the conditions under which it is raised, and Parker's thinks the improved meat quality is significant enough to keep several employees, a manager, and a veterinarian on its hog-farm payroll full-time.

Parker's barbecue is squarely in the eastern North Carolina mainstream: finely chopped; lightly sprinkled throughout with crushed red pepper flakes and seeds; and seasoned with salt, vinegar, and peppers. The relatively high proportion of white meat from the hams and loins makes this a fairly lean and dry barbecue, although it's served well moistened with sauce. Of course, there's always extra sauce on the table, and although Bobby Woodard calls his vinegar-and-pepper mixture "mild," there are enough red pepper flakes floating around in it to tip you off that this is not a condiment to be trifled with.

Boiled potatoes and a sweet, yellow coleslaw both help to soothe the palate between bites of liberally sauced barbecue, while the restaurant's golden corn sticks, which are baked and then deep fried, offer a satisfying heft and crunch in contrast to the soft textures of the other foods.

Another interesting taste contrast occurs between the tart, salty barbecue and Parker's thick Brunswick stew, which, according to eastern North Carolina tradition, is served very sweet. Now, you should realize that there are thousands of individuals and groups from this region who frequently cook their own large quantities of Brunswick stew, either as a hobby or as a fundraiser, mostly according to recipes handed down from one generation to the next. To these local chefs, who are invariably rigid about their methods of preparation, any restaurant stew is naturally going to be derided as institutional tasting at best, or—at worst—inedible. I have heard a lot of comments of this sort about Parker's stew, simply because the restaurant enjoys such a high visibility, but I personally think it's quite good—probably as good as you're going to find in any barbecue restaurant in the state.

Parker's fried chicken is also famous throughout this area of North Carolina, and the restaurant sells as much chicken as it does barbecue. Hundreds of churches, civic organizations, family reunions, and other groups within a fifty-mile range regularly place orders for large quantities of chicken, and that's not counting what's prepared and consumed through Parker's sizable catering operation. Parker's joins Bill's, The White Swan, and Bob Melton's in offering eastern North Carolina's finest fried chicken, and I would be hard-pressed to find anything negative to say about the chicken at any of these places, just as I would have trouble finding much of a difference in the way it's prepared at the various spots.

In terms of ambiance, Parker's is about as vanilla as it gets. The exterior is simple white clapboard, while the interior features sheet-paneled walls, Formica-topped tables, and no-nonsense wooden chairs. Parker's hires young men in high school and college to wait on tables—no waitresses—and they all wear white aprons and white-paper, drive-in-style hats as they scurry about with loaded food trays, lending an entirely appropriate '50s aura to the place.

Parker's is located on the southwest side of Wilson on U.S. 301, a short distance south of the intersection with U.S. 264. Open daily.

McCall's Barbecue and Seafood
Goldsboro

McCall's Barbecue and Seafood is a relative newcomer, having been in business only since 1989. However, it warrants mention because of the innovations the owners have employed to improve their product while maintaining the true spirit of pit-cooked barbecue.

Old friends Randy McCall and Worth Westbrook used to talk of owning their own business back when they both worked as feed salesmen for Ralston Purina. The two men ended up founding McCall's—although they did it in a rather unconventional way.

Back in the '70s, a man by the name of Elmer Davis had started a little one-day-a-week, pit-cooked barbecue business near the community of Pikeville, a few miles north of Goldsboro. (Pikeville is known as the birthplace of Charles B. Aycock, a former governor of North Carolina.) When Davis started his operation, he would take advance orders early each week for barbecued pork or chicken plates to be served on Friday, then go back to his pit and prepare the amount of each type food he needed to fill the orders. In many eastern North Carolina farming communities, popular foods such as chopped barbecue, fried fish, or barbecued chicken are often sold "by the plate" in this way—not only by enterprising individuals, but also by groups like the volunteer fire department, the PTA, or the local church. Around Goldsboro and Kinston, for example, fish stew is a favorite local delicacy, and before a particular batch is even prepared, it has often been completely sold—by the plate—in advance, with the orders to be filled between certain hours on a given day.

Davis's business prospered in a modest way, and the people around Pikeville began to really look forward to eating his barbecue on Fridays. Davis finally reached a point at which he had cooked several whole pigs and a number of chickens every Friday, week in and week out, for a period of several years. Meanwhile, McCall and Westbrook, who lived nearby, were looking around for a suitable business to enter. Randy McCall and his wife made the first move, figuring that if they took over Davis's part-time barbecue business, they could generate enough income for McCall's wife, who's an accountant, to be able to stay home one day a week.

The McCalls bought Davis's barbecue operation, and Worth Westbrook soon joined them in the business. After continuing to serve the Pikeville barbecue community for awhile, the partners decided to go full-time and expand. They bought an empty building just off U.S. 70 east of Goldsboro. The building had housed several other restaurant ventures, none of them successful. Their original concept was to open a new eatery featuring barbecue and seafood, with the barbecue to be pit cooked over oak coals at the small pit in Pikeville, then transported to the restaurant in Goldsboro. The building was renovated, and McCall's opened with a flourish in 1989. However, the restaurant's second day in business came close to being its last when the Pikeville barbecue pit caught fire and burned. (McCall and Westbrook ruefully admit that they managed to catch the pit on fire several times before this incident when they were basically selling barbecue to the Pikeville community, although they had previously suffered only minor damage.) The two partners were rescued by the nearby Nahunta volunteer fire department, which offered the use of its barbecue pits until Randy and Worth could rebuild.

What the two have installed since then is unlike anything else in North Carolina—or the nation, for that matter. In addition to constructing three conventional pits for cooking with hardwood coals out behind the restaurant, the partners also contracted with a midwestern firm, Old Hickory Pits, to modify a new cooker design to meet their needs. The invention consists of a Ferris wheel–type contraption of five baskets, each one containing five separate racks. Inside a ten-foot-square, stainless-steel oven, the "Ferris wheel" turns baskets loaded with either quartered pigs or chicken sections. In a cylindrical fire chamber that radiates heat at the back of the oven, gas flames combust either wood or charcoal (according to the operator's choice), and the smoke thus generated billows through vents in the fire chamber and into the oven where the loaded racks are rotating.

Quartered pigs are cooked for eleven hours in this cooker, then they're placed over oak coals on a conventional pit and cooked for another two hours. (The cooking times are different for chicken.) The results are excellent: the chopped, eastern North Carolina–style barbecue has a distinct wood-cooked flavor without being oversmoked, and the meat is as tender as could possibly be desired. (I'm told that any bone will pull cleanly from the meat by the time the pork quarters have finished slow cooking.) The barbecue is cooked fresh daily, and it is seasoned according to taste rather than predetermined measurements, "because every pig is different," says Westbrook. The partners point out that the pigs are intentionally cooked until they're a little on the dry side because their customers seem to prefer barbecue without a lot of moisture; although to my taste, it didn't seem at all too dry.

McCall's is a big, bustling restaurant, offering seafood and both a lunch and a dinner buffet in addition to barbecue plates and sandwiches. But don't let the size of McCall's fool you—the barbecue itself is reminiscent of the type you'd expect to find at a much smaller place.

Chopped pork barbecue is included on the buffet, along with barbecued chicken and a tray of pork skins and ribs; but because of the difficulty of holding peak flavor and texture in meat that's placed in a steam table for any length of time, I would recommend that you order your barbecue off the menu in order to enjoy it at its very freshest. The buffet does have an excellent selection of vegetables, as well as entrées such as pork chops and fried chicken.

For dessert, there's banana pudding with a meringue topping and peach cobbler made with an old-fashioned, biscuit-type crust, which some people prefer to the pie-pastry type.

McCall and Westbrook are to be commended for their commitment to stick with what is essentially pit-cooked barbecue in this relatively new restaurant, where it would have been far easier and less expensive to install gas or electric cookers. As it is, their barbecue is virtually indistinguishable from the best examples of whole-hog barbecue cooked entirely on a conventional pit, and the chicken turns out golden brown and tender, with a slight bit of charring offering eye appeal and an attractive crunchiness to the skin.

McCall and Westbrook have opened a second location at Cape Carteret. Their original restaurant is located about four-and-a-half miles east of Goldsboro at the intersection of U.S. 70 and N.C. 111. Headed east on U.S. 70, it's perhaps a half-mile past Wilber's Barbecue, on the opposite (north) side of the highway. The big, white, barn-shaped building is a good distance off the road, so keep your eyes peeled for the sign. Open daily.

Scott's Famous Barbecue
Goldsboro

Scott's is not one of those half-dozen or so places whose names spring immediately to the tongue whenever North Carolina barbecue is being discussed, but in fact, it's one of the state's oldest barbecue restaurant, as well as a thriving black-owned enterprise. Today, many of those who live outside Goldsboro are familiar with the family name through the visibility of Scott's Famous Barbecue Sauce, a quintessential eastern North Carolina style, vinegar-based sauce that's sold commercially in several grocery chains in North Carolina, South Carolina, and Virginia. The yellow label features the red silhouette of a pig and the legend: "It's The Best Ye Ever Tasted."

A portrait of the late Reverend Adam W. Scott hangs just inside the front door at Scott's Famous Barbecue in Goldsboro, and it's the image of a man with an intriguing twinkle in his eye. Scott was the founder of Scott's restaurant, a preacher in the Holiness Church, and the inventor of the sauce—well, sort of. Adam was a young man working as a janitor and elevator operator in Goldsboro when he first tried his hand at cooking barbecue. His early efforts were so enthusiastically received that he began to cater occasional parties and receptions, and a number of years later, he began regularly cooking pigs in a backyard pit on weekends and selling the meat. By 1933, he had enclosed the back porch of his home to make it into a dining room, and over the years, many of the state's most prominant citizens visited Scott's to sample some of his famous barbecue, including the late Governor J. Melvin Broughton.

An enigmatic aura just naturally surrounds any good barbecue man's sauce recipe, but Adam Scott perhaps carried the sense of mystery to new heights when he announced that the recipe for his sauce had come to him in a dream. That original recipe was served on Scott's barbecue for nearly thirty years, until Adam Scott's son, A. Martel Scott, Sr., spiced up the mixture a bit before obtaining a patent on the sauce in 1946. Since all eastern North Carolina barbecue sauces, including Scott's, start with a base of vinegar, salt, red pepper, and black pepper, what must have come to Adam Scott as he lay slumbering were all the ingredients which are lumped together on the label under the general classification of "spices." These spices form a two-inch sediment at the bottom of the reddish liquid before it's shaken thoroughly according to the directions on the label. In addition to several types of ground black and red pepper, there are some lighter-colored grains, something that might be onion or garlic powder . . . but then trying to guess the ingredients is really sort of pointless, the kind of game you play to pass the time while waiting in pleasant anticipation for your plate of barbecue to arrive. This is a robust, lively sauce that should be enjoyed for the sum of its parts, rather than any one or two ingredients. Suffice it to say that the overall taste sensation is of spicy, salty vinegar; that the coarse-ground pepper and spices impart a pleasant grittiness to the tongue, and that the heat is kept moderately under control. Personally, I enjoy taking an occasional swig straight from the bottle as I pass my kitchen pantry, and as for lifting a forkful of barbecue that's still glistening from an anointing of Scott's sauce—well, that *is* a dream-like experience.

In 1989, Scott's Famous Barbecue Sauce was awarded second place in a national competition among thirty-one vinegar-based barbecue sauces sponsored by *Food and Wine* magazine. Fewer than one-fourth of all the barbecue sauces on the market today are of the vinegar-based variety, so Scott's, in its award-winning eminence, stands as a lonely but sturdy reminder of eastern North Carolina's vinegar-flavored, barbecue heritage. Who knows: if this sauce had been available in the nineteenth century, maybe no one would ever have tried adding tomatoes to barbecue sauce.

While handing out well-deserved praise, we shouldn't forget that this stuff can blister your skin if you work around it too long without wearing rubber gloves. One night in 1957, someone saw a man breaking into Scott's restaurant and called the police. When the officers arrived and searched the premises, they found a broken window—but no burglar. As they were preparing to leave, they heard a sound from the storeroom, and when they investigated, they found the would-be thief hiding in a fifty-five-gallon drum half full of Scott's sauce. His rapidly growing discomfort had caused him to stir inside the barrel, which led to his discovery. The police lifted the man out of the drum and carted him off to jail, where he spent the night in a cell without benefit of a shower to wash the sauce from his skin and clothing. The next morning, Martel Scott showed up at the police station, and when he realized that the man had spent the night marinating in Scott's Famous Barbecue Sauce, he declined to press charges, saying the unfortunate intruder had already suffered enough.

Scott's has served its share of the rich and famous over the years. Adam Scott was invited to the White House on one occasion to serve barbecue to Franklin and Eleanor Roosevelt—he took along his children and even some of the grandchildren for the historic event. In the late '40s, Adam Scott turned the restaurant over to his son Martel, Sr., and moved to Winston-Salem to serve as the personal barbecue chef for R.J. Reynolds, Jr., Bob Hanes of Wachovia Bank, and James Hanes of the textile family. He continued traveling with the Reynolds' and cooking barbecue for high-society functions until 1976, when he returned to Goldsboro.

Adam died in 1983, but a third generation of Scotts operate the restaurant and sauce business. A. Martel Scott, Jr., is a quiet, modest man who seems to have a very different personality than the one you imagine his colorful grandfather must have had, but the continued successful operation of the family business was cause for Scott's to be featured in a 1992 article in *Entrepreneur* magazine.

Scott's is a cheerful, sunlight-filled place, with chrome-and-formica tables and comfortable booths upholstered in light green vinyl. The menu is fairly extensive—there are a lot of nonbarbecue items, along with a couple of unusual twists concerning the barbecue. For one thing, Scott's whole-hog barbecue is offered not only chopped, which in eastern North Carolina is *de rigueur*, but also sliced and "chunked" into tender, one-inch cubes. For another, barbecue plates are accompanied by a complimentary serving of crisp pork skin and a few ribs. (These are the ribs pulled from the roasted whole pig and are different from the spareribs offered on the menu.)

Scott's switched from hardwood to gas for cooking its barbecue around twenty years ago, so the meat has no smoky taste. On the other hand, both the white meat from the hams and loins, and the dark meat from the shoulders and sides is cooked for hours at the precisely-controlled low temperatures which are possible with gas cookers. This creates barbecue that is very moist and juicy. No sauce has been placed on the barbecue when it's brought to the table, so basically what you're being served is a very mild, naturally sweet, tender serving of roast pork, waiting to be turned into what the taste buds recognize as barbecue by a liberal dose of Scott's spirited Famous Barbecue Sauce. Think of the barbecue as the canvas and the sauce as the paint, and you'll leave Scott's having created a minor masterpiece.

The restaurant isn't highly visible to non-Goldsboro residents, although it's easy to find. From U.S. 70, which skirts the northern edge of Goldsboro, take the Williams Street exit and travel south toward town; you'll see the restaurant on the right. A square, yellow-and-red sign next to a small parking lot bears the same logo as the sauce label and announces Scott's Famous Barbecue. Judging by the modest dimensions of the sign, however, I figure the owners must assume everyone already knows how famous it is. Closed Sunday and Monday.

Wilber's Barbecue
Goldsboro

Wilber's is one of the biggest names in barbecue in eastern North Carolina, and unlike a few other famous places in the coastal plain, this is a restaurant where the name above the door still means *exactly* what it did thirty-four years ago when Wilber Shirley opened the place.

As far as I can determine, Wilber's is one of only four remaining restaurants anywhere in the eastern part of the state where barbecue is cooked entirely over hardwood coals. (The others are The Skylight Inn in Ayden, Bubba's at Cape Hatteras, and Moore's in New Bern.) Other places still trade on the names and the reputations of men who took the trouble to cook barbecue the old, slow way—the way it was meant to be cooked—but behind the scenes, their owners have quietly gotten rid of the wood, the pits, the smoke, the shovels, and the mess of pit cooking. Not Wilber. He points out that tradition comes with a hefty price tag, a fact he knows well, since he has a crew that cuts and splits wood year-round, but he says, "I think the finished product is worth the effort; I think that I've been successful with it, and I firmly believe that's the way to cook it."

There are larger barbecue operations if you count catering and wholesale distribution, but few, if any, barbecue restaurants in North Carolina serve more customers than Wilber's. And he not only manages to prepare his barbecue the old-fashioned way, he does it without seeming to make a big fuss about it. The fact that his staff will cook 130 entire pigs on a typical Labor Day weekend hasn't caused him to start looking anxiously into electric or gas cookers, and for that reason alone, lovers of real, pit-cooked barbecue ought to stop by his place and shake his hand.

The three most important things in real estate are location, location, *location*, and being well situated sure doesn't hurt in the barbecue business either. U.S. 70, which passes directly in front of Wilber's place east of Goldsboro, is usually clogged with day traffic between Raleigh and Kinston. But more importantly perhaps, it's also one of only three main routes to the ocean in North Carolina. Nearly everyone from the mountains, the western piedmont, the Triad, or the Triangle areas who is headed for Emerald Isle, Pine Knoll Shores, Atlantic Beach, Beaufort, Ocracoke, or Hatteras passes within thirty yards of Wilber's front door. Most of the military fighters at nearby Seymour Johnson Air Force Base also pass pretty close over his door, since the restaurant is located squarely beneath the landing pattern for the base. On more than one occasion after stepping out of my car in Wilber's parking lot, I've been startled out of my wits by a positively ground-shak-

ing, screaming blast from the tailpipe of some sweptwing fighter hurtling from out of nowhere directly over my head, a few hundred feet off the ground.

Beneath the continuing air show, Wilber's parking lot is nearly always crowded, especially during the vacation months when he usually allows someone to put up a produce stand right in front of the restaurant—you can eat lunch or dinner and pick up the fresh tomatoes, cucumbers, and peaches you'll need at the beach cottage all in one stop. I don't have any scientific basis for my belief that more vacation travelers stop at Wilber's on the way to the beach than do on the way home, but if that's true, then his enviable barbecue reputation would only be enhanced by the fact that the beachgoers have begun to unwind and get into that start-of-a-vacation euphoria by the time they walk through his door. It has to be easier to please customers who are in this pleasant state of mind.

Wilber's has a homey, laid-back feel to it: red brick and white trim on the outside, knotty pine paneling and red-checked tablecloths inside. There's a lunch counter and bustling takeout area in the center of the sprawling building, just inside the front door, with tables to the right and the left. Big, open dining rooms are located at either end of the building, allowing Wilber to seat more than three hundred at peak periods, which occur basically every Friday through Sunday. Plaques in the foyer ("South's Best Barbecue") and framed book excerpts and magazine articles hanging inside the restaurant provide quiet testimony to the reputation Wilber Shirley has built up among barbecue aficionados, not only in North Carolina, but across the country. But that reputation wasn't built inside the restaurant, which is, frankly, pretty ordinary looking. It came as the result of endless hours—long, slow, middle-of-the-night hours—at the barbecue pit out behind the main building.

The man who's put in most of those hours is sixty-six-year-old Ike Green, a patient, affable man who's been cooking pigs for Wilber Shirley for twenty-eight years now. Green's domain encompasses a one-hundred-foot woodpile, an open-air fireplace with a straight wooden chair pulled up beside it, and a long cinder-block building with hip-high, open pits running the length of each side. Each evening, just a hundred yards or so from the eighteen-wheelers that roar up and down U.S. 70, Green builds a fire of stacked oak logs in the fireplace. He lets the fire burn down to coals for an hour or so as he trundles a wheelbarrow back and forth between the pit house and the restaurant building, loading the fifty-six half-pigs he'll cook that night onto the pits, where they'll slow-roast for nine hours.

On a cool evening, having straightened the last side of pork on the cooking grate, and waiting for the fire to burn down a bit more,

Green pulls the straight-backed chair up to the fire, rares back on the spindly rear legs, and reflects on his beginnings in the pig-cooking business. It seems that when he was around thirteen years old, Green went to an older friend's house one evening during the Christmas holidays to help him cook a pig on a backyard pit dug into the ground. The older man drank too much and went to sleep, but young Ike stayed up all night tending the coals. When the man's wife came out the next morning to inspect, she pronounced the cooked pig "pretty" and praised the dogged teenager for the good job he had done. "You give a child praise and he'll think he's done something great," Ike rumbles, "and that's what started me cookin' 'em, and I've been cookin' 'em ever since."

Green glances at the fire, straightens up from the chair, and picks up a shovel leaning against the pit-house wall. He raps the burning logs with the back of the shovel to break them up and cause the embers to fall to the bottom of the fireplace, then pushes the flat implement into the red-orange mound, straightening up with a shovel full of flickering coals. Trailing sparks, he walks with an unhurried pace across the hard-packed dirt and into the pit house, stopping at the nearest pit. Pushing back a low, sliding door, he inserts the shovel through the opening and scatters the embers in a perfectly even cascade beneath the meat lying two feet above. He then walks back outside and over to the fire-place, scrapes up another shovel full of coals, and repeats the process, trudging steadily back and forth for twenty minutes between the fire and the increasingly smoky pit house as he works his way down the pits to the end of the building. Then, leaning his shovel back against the wall, he moves slowly to his chair and eases himself down.

"I like sittin' out here, takin' my time," he says quietly. "There ain't nobody much to bother you. Once in a while, somebody'll come along actin' strange, and I'll send them on their way. But if somebody comes by and acts right, I'll sit and talk with him. When I get the pigs done and turn 'em, maybe I'll give him a rib. But I can't work if I got to watch somebody too close."

What's going to happen to Wilber Shirley when Green retires or gets too old to keep it all up? "Well, he might have to close up," says Green with perfect seriousness, "because he likely ain't going to get nobody . . . I mean I haven't seen nobody yet from this younger generation . . . that's faithful, you know, and will work and stay right here with it like I do."

That, friends, will be the epitaph for a lot of barbecue places one of these days.

Wilber Shirley himself is no slouch when it comes to hard work. He's usually at the restaurant twelve or thirteen hours a day, six days a week, but he says that after thirty-four years of owning this place (and several years spent working for the former Griffin's Barbecue in Goldsboro before that), he still loves coming to work every morning. He has a son-in-law who's been with the business for twenty years now, so he's hopeful the operation can remain in family hands. If I were in his shoes, I think I would find some young man who wanted to stay close to home and pay him about forty thousand dollars a year to become an apprentice to Ike Green, making it well worth his while to put up with the long, night hours and the hot, back-aching work. It seems like a lot of money—but then, what's a reputation worth?

In any case, since you never know what's going to happen, I advise you to enjoy Wilber's tender, juicy, wood-smoked barbecue while you can and for as long as you can. Shirley says he thinks eastern-style barbecue is unique because it combines several parts of the pig, all with slightly different tastes and textures. "It's kind of like making a cake with different ingredients," he observes. "You mix meat from the hams, the shoulders, the loin, and the side, and all of them are a little bit different, so you end up with a blend." He makes his particular blend a little more moist than some whole-hog chopped barbecue by adding extra dark meat from several shoulders he's barbecued on the side, and this innovation also allows him to include more shreds of dark brown, chewy, outside meat, making the mixture appealing to the eye as well as the palate. In my opinion, most eastern North Carolina barbecue houses end up with too fine a texture for their barbecue by using machines to chop it, but Wilber's still does this time-honored task by hand, which helps maintain the moisture of the meat and provides a pleasingly chunky texture.

Wilber's barbecue is seasoned to taste with salt and ground pepper after it's chopped, but most people will want to add a splash of his special sauce, which is served in cruets at the table and is also for sale, bottled, at the cash register. Like all eastern sauces, it contains vinegar, salt, red pepper, black pepper, and spices (the mystery ingredients), but Wilber's sauce is, perhaps, the most complex blend of this general type that I've tasted. Several unknown earth-toned spices give the sauce an unusual reddish brown shade. I believe there are several distinct varieties of finely ground, dried red peppers in the sauce, but the taste, while lively, is spicy and flavorful, not searingly hot. Wilber's is one of several eastern sauces that needs frequent shaking to loosen and blend the extremely fine sediment of spices that settles to the bottom of the bottle, like minute grains of sand settling on a riverbed.

Of all the barbecue places I've visited across North Carolina, I've never been to any others besides Wilber's that serve potato salad with barbecue. Not that there's anything unusual about potato salad in this region; it's just that it's usually served with a cold meat, like sliced, boiled ham. Although it's a little jarring to see it sitting on a plate beside a serving of barbecue, the potato salad is quite good, featuring a smoother consistency and more of a vinegar bite than some recipes.

Wilber's serves combination plates, featuring barbecue and either fried or pit-barbecued chicken, along with the potato salad, Brunswick stew, coleslaw, and hush puppies. There are even some seafood selections available, as well. These side offerings all get high marks for quality and consistency, but the main thing you'll remember after a visit to Wilber's is the barbecue itself, which is absolutely superb.

Wilber's is located four miles east of Goldsboro on U.S. 70. Open daily.

The White Swan
Smithfield

The White Swan is one of those tiny, unprepossessing places off the beaten track that you're always really smug about discovering. Of course, it's only off the beaten track for those who don't live around the Smithfield area, and not far off the track at that: just a mile-and-a-half from Interstate 95. For area residents, though, it's not only a place with consistently delicious eastern-style barbecue,

NORTH CAROLINA BARBECUE : *Flavored by Time*

superb fried chicken, and championship-caliber hush puppies—it's a place with a colorful past . . . a reputation.

Having hopefully established the White Swan's gastronomic credentials up front, I want to tell you a little about the history of the place before getting down to the details of the dining experience. You'll enjoy sitting in the tiny, wood-paneled dining room, sipping some truly wonderful ice tea, and anticipating the arrival of your order as you let the flavor of the spot soak in while you imagine the Swan in its earlier days.

Just across the parking lot from the present barbecue restaurant stood the infamous Flowers' Tavern, a two-story roadhouse and tourist court dating back to the late '20s. It was apparently sort of a Tennessee Williams kind of place, and you can almost hear the duet between the faint, bluesy wail of a saxophone and the rhythmic humming of the cicadas as you imagine what the place might have been like on a sultry summer evening:

Dark automobiles huddle untidily in the building's shadow, their windshields and chrome bumpers reflecting the bright red and blue of a flashing neon sign. Pale golden rectangles of light fall from the windows and cut sharply across a dusty parking lot, and from inside, the insistent thump of the drums is the only fragment of the jukebox's blare that manages

to cut through a discordant babble of voices and the clink of glasses. From the dusky gloom comes the "chunk" of a car door opening, and a deep, rich female laugh floats through the purple evening and across the dark highway, disappearing into the black cloak of the woods.

Ava Gardner, the movie star, grew up and is buried in Smithfield, and you can easily combine an excursion to the White Swan with a visit to the Ava Gardner museum downtown. Even before she became famous, the raven-haired beauty with the throaty voice is said to have had a fondness for night life, and you can't help wondering whether the Flowers joint may have been one of the spots she frequented. There's no evidence of that, but the rumors fly thick and fast, even today, that Flowers' Tavern was widely known for the availability of bootleg whiskey and, well, female companionship.

In 1951, Cleveland Holly bought the place and tore down all but four of the sixteen tourist-court cabins that stood in a row along U.S. 301, then one of the main north-south routes through eastern North Carolina. He replaced the freestanding cabins with a long, one-story brick motel and demolished the second story of the old tavern building, remodeling the ground floor into a brick-veneered restaurant. Most importantly, he changed the name of the place to the White

Swan, perhaps thinking of the large number of these graceful birds that can be found in the swamps surrounding the Neuse River and nearby Holt Lake. Holly later built a small barbecue-pit building a few feet from the restaurant, and for years, diners could choose between a hearty, country-type meal in the dining room or barbecue and hush puppies next door at the pit. Holly lived in the motel, which he operated along with the restaurant and barbecue stand until his death in 1977. Evidently he distrusted banks, because on the morning he died peacefully in his sleep, the accumulated cash earnings of many years were found stashed all around his lodgings. Following Holly's death, the Swan was taken over by a brother-in-law, who is credited with adding fried chicken to the barbecue-pit menu.

In 1988, the business was bought by Lynwood Parker, a Smithfield accountant, and one of his clients, J.D. Heath. Parker and Heath added a small dining room to the barbecue-pit building, created a catering business, and expanded the menu to include Brunswick stew, baked beans, and boiled potatoes, all of which are White Swan staples today. Heath died in 1994, and Parker continues to operate the Swan in partnership with Heath's widow, Katie.

The original restaurant is now open only for breakfast, although it's also available for civic club meetings or family gatherings. Meanwhile, the expanded barbecue stand next door is a bustling business. In addition to a couple of tables in the original eating area, there is seating for thirty in the intimate dining room, a cheerful place with a varnished wood ceiling and walls, and curved wood-slat benches. Despite the limited seating, Parker says the restaurant serves from six hundred to one thousand people a day, thanks in part to a healthy take-out business.

Lynwood Parker—at this writing the mayor *pro tempore* of Four Oaks and a past chairman of the Johnston County G.O.P.—answers with the smoothness of a veteran politician when asked why the White Swan quit cooking its barbecue over hardwood coals and began using electric cookers. It seems, says Parker with a completely straight face, that some of his customers were complaining about the smoky taste of the barbecue. With this kind of audacity, Parker could obviously move smoothly into a higher elective office, but I have to admit that the White Swan is one of those rare places where the barbecue seems to suffer very little from the transition. While I never had the opportunity to taste the work of Raymond Massengill, the veteran Swan pit man who shoveled oak and hickory coals at the restaurant for forty-one years, I found the modern, electric-cooked version soft and moist, yet crunchy—with brown outside bits and an attractive, if mild, seasoning. The White Swan is one of only two places I have run across that, as an added attraction, routinely garnish a barbecue plate with a crunchy, brown piece of fried pork skin, a toothsome accompaniment to the tender chopped meat.

The house barbecue sauce is a hot, salty vinegar mixture, and the average diner will want to add a few dashes to his serving of chopped barbecue. A United States senator who is a frequent customer once ordered a bottle of the sauce to take home. Not wanting to take advantage of his position, the senator insisted on paying for the bottle; but ever since then, he's been ragging Parker unmercifully about charging him five dollars for "fifteen cents worth of vinegar and pepper."

The Swan's coleslaw is eastern style, lightly dressed with mayonnaise and appealingly sprinkled through with bits of chopped sweet pickle.

You won't be able to stay out of the basket of hush puppies they bring to your table at the Swan. Some reviewers have pronounced them the best they've ever eaten, and they certainly deserve to be up there at the top of anyone's list. They're extremely light, crispy, and faintly sweet, with that perfect golden brown color that results from years of frying experience, along with oil that's heated to an exact temperature. Oddly enough, Parker is quick to mention that the hush puppies are made from an Atkinson's Mills mix that's available in area stores. If you can cook them half as well as the ladies at the Swan do, my hat's off to you.

Fried chicken is a popular accompaniment to barbecue in the coastal plain, and to me, there are only three or four places down east that manage to keep it moist and juicy inside, with a crisp, perfectly browned skin. The White Swan is one of them. This is not one of those extra-crispy, batter-type coatings that showers crumbs everywhere as you bite into the chicken. If you pinch off a bite of this chicken, the rest of the piece stays together; the inside meat is as flavorful as the skin; and there's no greasy feel to the chicken at all. They must be doing something right: the White Swan cooks from six hundred to one thousand chickens a week, which is a lot for a restaurant with such a limited seating capacity.

Parker says the secret to the White Swan's popularity is "consistency with people who like your barbecue." I've stopped at the White Swan on several occasions and have found that the offerings are, indeed, consistently good. The owners have recently opened a second White Swan location on U.S. 70 in Princeton, and a third location is being contemplated; but for now, all the barbecue will be prepared at the original Smithfield location. To get there, take I-95 south to Exit 90, then go a mile-and-a-half toward Smithfield on U.S. 301/N.C. 96 North. You'll see the White Swan's distinctive sign and white painted building on your left. Open daily.

Stephenson's Barbecue
Willow Spring

First of all, you may have trouble finding the Wake County community of Willow Spring on a map. Second, a lot of maps spell it Willow *Springs*, which the post office swears is wrong. Third, Stephenson's, except for mail delivery purposes, isn't even in Willow Spring, but is really located some ten miles away in Johnston County. Actually the restaurant is smack in the middle of a rural no man's land where the borders of Wake, Harnett, and Johnston Counties join, about halfway between Benson and Garner, and midway between Fuquay-Varina and Smithfield. But regardless of its being well off the beaten track, Stephenson's is usually packed at lunch and dinner, and that tells you pretty much everything you need to know right up front.

Back in the mid-'50s, Paul Stephenson was a farmer and didn't have any barbecue experience. One day, a man showed up and bought fourteen of his hogs for eleven cents a pound. "I got to thinking . . . who's making the money on these pigs?," Stephenson remembers. "He was going to chop 'em up into sandwiches and come out smelling like roses, and I decided I'd a whole lot rather smell like roses than what I smelled like at the time, so I really started thinking hard about getting into the barbecue business."

In due time, Stephenson managed to get himself out of farming and into the business of serving the public, and the new restaurant seemed like the perfect place to teach the values Stephenson wanted to pass along to his young family. When Paul's two sons, Andy and Wayne, were growing up and playing baseball, their father convinced them that chopping barbecue would build up their hand and arm muscles, giving them more heat on their fastball and a better break on their curve. The two obviously embraced that notion wholeheartedly, because the center of the restaurant's old butcher block, now on display in the restaurant's vestibule, is hollowed out like a wooden bowl from all the spirited barbecue chopping it absorbed. The training must have worked pretty well since Wayne went on to become an all-state high school pitcher.

That early chopping has paid off for Andy, too. After several years of working in the family nursery business adjacent to the restaurant (which Wayne now operates), he's joined his father in running Stephenson's Barbecue. Andy's wife Lynn has also assumed a major role at the restaurant. "The best thing about our restaurant," Lynn says, "is the family atmosphere among the owners, workers, and customers. We're down to earth, and the people who eat here are too." Paul Stephenson, who's "Mr. Paul" to the staff, is talking about retiring, but he still shows up most days, often accompanied by his wife Ann, to look things over and chat with his friends—who are also his customers—in the dining room. Most of the kitchen workers have been at Stephenson's for many years, and while tending the heavy pork shoulders on the hot, smoky pits has always been considered a man's job, the ladies in the kitchen have been responsible for the home-cooked vegetables and the weekly specials, like spareribs and chicken-and-pastry, that have made Stephenson's famous in the area.

Stephenson's uses hardwood charcoal in its pits, rather than oak or hickory coals, and both Paul and Andy are convinced that the charcoal actually gives the meat a smokier flavor and better taste than could be attained from wood. The pork shoulders are cooked during the day, and Paul Stephenson says he's learned that the meat absorbs an extra measure of wood-smoked taste if it's left on the pits overnight as the charcoal briquettes slowly burn out.

Even though it's prepared from pork shoulders rather than the whole hog, the barbecue here is eastern-style in its salt, vinegar, and pepper seasoning, even if it isn't as finely chopped as some of the barbecue you'll find in the region. Paul and Andy tend to chop the lean, light-colored chunks of what they call "beautiful meat" from the shoulder fairly coarsely, while the crusty, brown outside layer is more finely chopped to add flavor and texture throughout the mixture. A very small amount of fat, scraped from the inside of the skin, is also added, since this is where most of the wood-smoked flavor is concentrated, but by anyone's standards, this is still very lean barbecue. The typical Stephenson's barbecue plate is accompanied by coleslaw, boiled potatoes in a mild, tomato-flavored base, and hush puppies with a touch of onion, all well prepared and appetizing.

As good as the barbecue is at Stephenson's, you'll be missing out if you don't also explore some of the other menu offerings. Neither the barbecued chicken (prepared every day) nor the pork ribs (prepared Thursday through Saturday) are pit cooked, but they are slowly roasted in the oven, each smothered in its own flavorful, tomato-based sauce, until the meat can easily be cut with a fork alone. These specialties are available with a wide range of country-style vegetables, depending on the season.

But to enjoy Stephenson's biggest hit, aside from the barbecue, you'll want to seek out the restaurant on a Thursday—the one day of the week on which "Miss Louise" has prepared her chicken-and-pastry for nearly thirty years. Stewing hens are slowly cooked in a large pot, then removed from the stock so that the skin and bones can be removed. The chicken is then shredded, added back into the delicious broth, and layered with strips of Miss Louise's hand-rolled pastry. If, after sampling this dish, you decide that you intend to marry Miss Louise on the spot, you may have quite a battle on your hands from her other well-fed admirers.

Stephenson's is a simple, cheerful place, with red-checked tablecloths, where all the food is served on real plates, rather than on paper or plastic, as is the custom in most barbecue restaurants. Picture windows opening onto a well-landscaped garden area add a peaceful touch to the larger of two dining rooms, but a thriving trade has pushed Stephenson's seating capacity to the limit, and peak periods can be a little hectic. There's talk of expansion, but in the meantime, the quality of the food and the friendly atmosphere are worth any crowded conditions you might encounter.

Stephenson's is located on N.C. 50, some twenty miles south of Raleigh, but the easiest access is via Interstate 40. From the Triangle area, take I-40 East toward Benson. Take Exit 319 (McGee's Crossroads) and drive west on N.C. 210 to its intersection with N.C. 50. Turn right (north) on N.C. 50 and keep an eye out for Stephenson's Barbecue on the right side. Closed Sunday.

Bob's Barbecue
Creedmore

When Nita Whitfield and her husband Bobby built Bob's Barbecue in 1970, it seemed way out in the country, several miles outside Creedmore. At that time, Interstate 85 hadn't been completed in the Creedmore-Butner area, twelve miles north of Durham, but the Whitfields knew it soon would be—and today, Bob's location on N.C. 56 is just a couple of hundred yards from the busy north-south artery. With the arrival of the interstate, the whole region has become a busy center of commerce. The entire area around Exit 191 has filled up with several motels, a strip shopping center, and all the major fast-food franchises. The community of Butner, just down the road, has experienced virtually constant expansion in recent years due to the presence of a state mental hospital, a center for the mentally retarded, an alcohol-treatment facility, and a federal prison; and several new plants and corporate campuses have been built in the area. And it seems that the people who work at these places are all fond of eating at Bob's Barbecue, where they mingle with a steady stream of I-85 travelers and the construction workers who are widening the highway.

The joint, as they say, is jumpin'.

"They love our food . . . and we're fast," says Louise Blevins, the lady who's been making Bob's homemade pies for the past sixteen years. "Most of them don't have but thirty minutes for lunch, counting traveling time, but they can come in here and get something really good to eat and still make it back to work on time." Customers at Bob's pick up a tray and go through a mini-cafeteria line. Barbecue and side dishes are served up on the spot, while orders for hamburgers, seafood, and other menu selections go back to the kitchen and are delivered to the table.

Bob's is actually named for Nita's father, Bob Whitt, who died in 1985. A longtime deputy sheriff in nearby Roxboro, Whitt opened a barbecue stand there relatively late in life and ran it for some fifteen years before retiring. But retirement didn't really suit Whitt, so his only daughter Nita and her husband built the present restaurant—basically to give her father something to do. Bob Whitt ran the place for ten years until his health began to fail, and now Nita handles most of the responsibilities of operation, with occasional input from her husband. She has two young men to take care of the meat and a mostly female staff to prepare and serve the rest of the food, and she says she probably has the best group of workers in Granville County. One thing's for sure: the employees are proud of the restaurant. One longtime

staffer pulled me aside and looked me straight in the eye as she asked, "You do understand? This place is an institution."

Nita says that before her father opened his Roxboro place in 1957, he went all over the state researching various methods of cooking barbecue; and at the outset, Bob Whitt decided to go with an electric pit rather than messing with wood. He bought one of the first electric pits anywhere in the area. The pork shoulders at Bob's are still cooked that way, although the original cooker has long since been replaced. If there have been any complaints about the lack of a wood-smoked taste in this barbecue, they certainly haven't seemed to affect the restaurant's popularity. I've been contacted by several people who wanted to recommend the place, and one fellow from Virginia told me it was his favorite North Carolina barbecue restaurant.

The barbecue at Bob's is hand-chopped, tender, and fresh tasting, and it comes to the table already well moistened by a mild, sweet sauce that contains very little evidence of pepper. No skin or fat are chopped up into the barbecue, so you're basically getting pure, lean meat. This is good, solid, middle-of-the-road 'cue, prepared according to Bob Whitt's carefully considered way of doing things, and it's the kind of barbecue that would win awards for consistently pleasing taste rather than for excitement. And let's face it: there are a lot of people who would tell you that excitement is the last thing they want to encounter in any restaurant, especially in a barbecue place. The barbecue is accompanied by a mild, pleasing mayonnaise-based coleslaw and fresh, crisp hush puppies.

Brunswick stew is a big deal at Bob's. They make it up forty gallons at a time, four or five days a week. When customers walk up to the serving counter to place their order, the first thing they see is a couple of pots of Brunswick stew, sitting at the ready in pans of simmering water on an electric range, which is the way Nita Whitfield's veterans prefer to serve the stew, rather than from a steam tray. The mixture is sweet and perfectly seasoned, although in my judgment, it could stand to be just a slight bit thicker. Chicken, pork, and beef are all used in this recipe, but the vegetables are limited—as they properly should be—to tomatoes, potatoes, butter beans, cream-style corn, and onions. Thankfully, there are no green beans, garden peas, okra, or any of the dozens of other extraneous ingredients that often find their way into the so-called Brunswick stew found in the piedmont.

Bob's is another of those places that sit on or near the dividing line between two schools of thought regarding barbecue. In response to my question, Nita said she wasn't sure whether Creedmore is located in the east or piedmont (I'm not sure myself), and there's

an interesting blend of the two regional styles at Bob's. Piedmont-style pork shoulders are accompanied by mayonnaise-based slaw and Brunswick stew, which are both ordinarily confined to the eastern region, and no one seems to find the anomaly the slightest bit unusual.

Another of the restaurant's specialties that's known far and wide is homemade chicken salad, which is made from Nita's mother-in-law's recipe. As you might expect, the salad is often purchased in large quantities for bridesmaid's luncheons, teas, and other predominantly female social gatherings. Louise Blevins says between eight and twelve large stewing hens are simmered every day until the meat is ready to drop off the bones, and they make the salad in pots so big that she has to stand on tiptoe to see inside. This chicken salad has a substantial consistency—containing hand-chopped, boned chicken meat rather than the minced or pulverized stuff that goes into commercial chicken salad—so in addition to being a popular standard for ladies' events, it's plenty hearty for a man's appetite, too.

The thing at Bob's that will stick in your memory more than anything else, though, is homemade pie. Chocolate-cream pie. Chocolate-chess pie. Sweet-potato pie. Forty to fifty pies a day . . . all made right on the premises by Louise Blevins. In September, when Bob's obtains its yearly supply of sweet potatoes,

NORTH CAROLINA BARBECUE : *Flavored by Time*

Nita, Louise, and the other staffers peel some sixty bushels of sweet potatoes to go into the pie filling mixture, which is prepared, then frozen. There are eight large chest freezers at Bob's, and a good deal of the space in those freezers is taken up by sweet-potato pie filling. Apparently, if you work at Bob's, you do not want to run out of sweet potato pie. "If we give out of that, we might as well just pack it up and go home," says Blevins, shaking her head in awe and fear at the very thought. "People get angry if you tell them you're out . . . not just irritated . . . angry!"

At present, Bob's seats only 150 people, which really isn't enough considering the traffic. Nita says she knows she really ought to expand, but adds, "I'm just too tired." She has one married daughter who helps out in the restaurant from time to time, but Nita says it's too early to tell whether the daughter and her husband will be interested in taking over the restaurant one day.

Getting to Bob's Barbecue is easy: Simply take Exit 191 (the Butner-Creedmore exit) from Interstate 85 some twelve miles north of Durham, then turn east toward Creedmore. The restaurant is on your left, approximately two hundred yards from the interchange. Nita Whitfield says she doesn't intend to keep anyone from going to church, so the restaurant is closed on Sunday. You may also want to avoid their busiest day, Friday, when five different groups meet at the restaurant.

Allen & Son Barbecue
Chapel Hill

What makes a guy like Keith Allen keep the faith? There isn't a man in North Carolina who works any harder to produce superb barbecue, and the fact that he's never quite reaped the financial rewards or basked in the praise afforded some other, better-known restaurateurs has never deterred him from his single-minded purity of purpose. No shortcuts. "This business of cooking barbecue has to be done a certain way—it has to be done *right*," he insists. "When we get so that we can't do it the right way, we'll just pull the name off the sign and go home."

Allen stands about six-foot-three and has the shoulders of a frontiersman, broad enough to carry the burden of doing what others will not do in his pursuit of excellence. Almost any barbecue man will tell you that the hickory wood required to slow-cook pork to perfection is increasingly hard to find. Allen came to that realization twenty years ago, so he started searching for the wood and cutting and hauling it himself, a brutally demanding labor of love that continues today. That still leaves the chore of reducing the pile of hickory logs he accumulates out back— tree trunks, really—into pieces small enough to work with.

"We split it ourselves," says David Turner,

117

x

North Carolina Barbecue Restaurants

Keith Allen of Chapel Hill splits his own hickory.

Allen's right-hand man and chief cook.

"With what," I wanted to know, "a log splitter?"

"Yeah—this is our log splitter right here," Turner chuckles, picking up a steel wedge and a maul—a cross between an ax and a sledgehammer. You see who we're dealing with here? Two guys who cut and split their barbecue-cooking wood *by hand*. And once it's split, they gather it up by the armful and carry it twenty or thirty feet to the big fireplace between the two pits, where the forty-inch sections burn down into coals suitable for shoveling periodically beneath the cooking meat.

There have been a couple of other places bearing the Allen & Son name, but the rather unprepossessing site on N.C. 86, some six miles north of Chapel Hill toward Hillsborough, is the spot where the real art is created. The original Allen & Son restaurant, founded by Keith's father, is located on U.S. 15-501 south of Chapel Hill near Bynum. It's now leased-out under separate management, serving electrically-cooked barbecue. A former Allen & Son location on N.C. 54, just south of Interstate 85 at Graham, has been closed for several years. "We just couldn't cook with wood and keep all the places open—it's too much work," says Keith Allen. "We decided to concentrate on really doing it right at this one place."

Allen worked in the original restaurant as a youngster, and he was attending UNC-Chapel Hill and working part-time as a meat cutter when he heard that the former Turner's Barbecue was for sale. "I came out, looked around, and bought this place on my lunch hour from the A&P," he remembers, "and then I went back and told my father that I had a barbecue place, too." He's been there twenty-five years, and while the location on N.C. 86 between Chapel Hill and Hillsborough is not exactly prime in terms of traffic, Allen has built up a nice business between the restaurant and an active catering operation focusing on pig pickings.

The propane-gas tanks on Allen's portable barbecue cookers might lead his party patrons to the erroneous conclusion that he has opted for this easier cooking method, but in fact, the gas burners simply serve to keep the barbecued pigs warm at the catering site. In this crossover area between east and piedmont, whole or half hogs are still in demand for catered "pig pickings": they're lovingly cooked over pure hickory coals on the restaurant's pit, along with the pork shoulders preferred for the chopped barbecue served in the restaurant. Both are usually tended by Turner, a lifelong cook who works with an innovative roll-out rack which greatly simplifies the task of turning the meat during the cooking process. Some barbecuers like to mix a little green hickory or oak with their dry wood, but Turner is strictly a dry-wood man. He likes to shovel in and smooth out his first bed of coals of the day and get the pit very hot before he ever rolls the rack containing the meat over the embers. From then on, he sprinkles coals sparingly under the shoulders—around every thirty minutes—and because the pit is preheated, his pork is usually falling off the bone in around seven hours. While the shoulders are transformed almost instantly into chopped, seasoned barbecue while they're still smoking hot from the pit, a roasted whole or half hog for a pig picking must present an attractive, appetizing appearance to the party guests. It's here that Turner displays the fruits of his years of experience, proudly pulling from the pit's smoky darkness a crusty, mahogany-hued side of pork without a single charred spot, guaranteed to delight even the most hard-eyed judge of the barbecuer's craft.

Allen & Son occupies the corner of a wooded lot, a small cinder-block building with a graveled parking lot and a weathered metal sign. The interior decor is a bit weathered, as well, but comfortable, with cream-colored walls, dark green tablecloths, and touches of pine paneling. The menu contains quite a few nonbarbecue items, including fried seafood, homemade hamburgers (served Carolina-style, with chili, slaw, mustard, and onion), and daily specials, like homemade meat loaf. The barbecue plates—chopped barbecue, coleslaw, and hush puppies—are available with or without french fries, but I recommend you order your meal *with* because they aren't the usual frozen steak fries or crinkle cuts. Instead, wonder of wonders, they're the real thing: homemade, chunky, skins-on strips cut from large baking-type potatoes and deep fried to a wonderful shade of brown that's about thirty seconds past the "golden" stage.

The generous mound of glistening fries spilling off the plate is reason enough for a trip to Allen & Son, but they're just a warmup for the barbecue, which is coarsely chopped into meltingly tender chunks, sprinkled through with shreds of deep brown, chewy outside meat—not skin. The wood-smoke taste from pure hickory seems to be a touch darker and more intense than that from other hardwoods such as oak, and Allen's barbecue has a manly robustness without being overly smoky. The peppery sauce mixed into the chopped meat before it's served is thin, dark red, and slightly sweet, but the tang of the vinegar is softened by a slight touch of melted butter or shortening, giving the barbecue an attractive, slightly shiny glaze.

It's worth mentioning that Keith Allen has the most aggressive barbecue-chopping style I've ever witnessed. Working with insulated rubber gloves, Allen and Turner carry the shoulders from the pits to the kitchen and quickly strip steaming-hot meat from five or six shoulders at a time, until there's a pyramid of pork chunks perhaps three feet across and a foot high. Seizing two machete-shaped cleavers called "lamb breakers"—slightly longer and narrower than the usual barbecue-chopping implement—Allen plants his feet in a wide stance and begins chopping with both arms in a rapid, rhythmic cadence, never slowing or faltering until the entire mound of meat has been turned into chopped barbecue ready for seasoning. Whether from weightlifting or years of handling the heavy steel cleavers, Allen's arms and shoulders are thickly muscled, and it takes him only a few minutes to chop an entire day's supply of barbecue.

Allen serves one of the tastiest and most authentic versions of Brunswick stew that I've run across. I've never liked most of the Brunswick stew sold in the piedmont, especially the stuff sold by churches and other fundraising groups, although I usually buy it just to be supportive. To my way of thinking, far too many extraneous meats and vegetables—mostly canned—often find their way into these free-spirited concoctions. But Allen stays with the traditional ingredients: chicken and/or pork, tomatoes, potatoes, corn, and lima beans. His stew is properly thick and

satisfying, and the vegetables are not cooked into an unidentifiable mush as is often the case. Brunswick stew is often slightly sweet, usually because of the use of cream-style corn, but Allen's version is straightforward meat-and-vegetables, with no detectable added sugar. I like it either way, and his recipe offers a slight but interesting change from the stew that's a common side dish in barbecue houses east of Raleigh.

Don't fill up on hush puppies at Allen & Son. In the first place, they're OK, but nothing really extraordinary. In the second place, even if they were at the absolute zenith of the deep fryer's art, they still wouldn't hold a candle to Keith Allen's delectable homemade desserts. Most barbecue places I've visited offer banana pudding and fruit cobblers, and there are some truly outstanding examples of each around the state, but Allen's dessert list is unique. I sampled pecan pie with a perfect flaky crust and a rich, moist, not-too-sticky filling that was obviously freshly made. The pie was topped with a scoop of homemade vanilla ice cream that had that delightfully icy, almost grainy texture assuring me that only fresh milk, cream, eggs, sugar, and vanilla went into it, not the tree sap known as guar gum or xanthan gum that commercial ice cream producers include to produce a bland, phony smoothness. Allen also has cream cheese pound cake (with cream cheese icing), chess and blueberry pie, cobblers, and a sel-dom-seen item that's one of my personal fa-vorites at home: bread pudding—moistened bread baked into a rich custard, with plenty of plump, juicy raisins.

If Keith Allen was interested in volume or profits alone, he would have opted out of the barbecue business long ago; in fact, he has other business interests which allow him to keep cooking barbecue in the time-hon-ored way he loves. Any barbecue lover who likes to pass along a nod of appreciation for hard work and tradition should make this a regular stopping place. Allen & Son is just a couple of minute's drive off Interstate 40, not far from its intersection with Interstate 85 near Hillsborough. From I-40, take the N.C. 86 exit and turn north; you'll find Allen & Son a mile-and-a-half down the road on the left side, just before a railroad crossing. Closed Sunday.

Hursey's Barbecue
Burlington

Charles Hursey believes he's single-handedly chopped more barbecue than any other North Carolinian. According to Hursey, if the pork shoulders he's chopped were placed end to end, they would stretch from Hursey's home base in Burlington to Cin-cinnati, Ohio, and provide enough meat to fill seventy million barbecue sandwiches. Fur-thermore, he invites anyone who wants to challenge his assertion to bring their facts and figures over to his restaurant and argue their case over a glass of what he claims is the best ice tea in town; he'll pick up the tab on the tea for anyone who proves him wrong.

Actually, Hursey's claims arise mostly from the nearly forty years he's spent in the barbe-cue wholesale business servicing restaurants, supermarkets, and institutional customers, both directly and through several major meat distributors. He didn't really have what could be called a high-profile barbecue restaurant until 1985, when he opened up his place on the corner of South Church Street and Alamance Road in Burlington. There, from atop a knoll, the smoke from Hursey's wood-fired pits and the enchanting aroma of roasting pork float down over a busy in-tersection, mesmerizing drivers with im-ages of savory barbecue and causing them to turn obediently into the parking lot in front of Hursey's cheerful, country-style brick building. Inside, the photographs, newspaper articles, and awards displayed around the foyer reflect the family's four generations in the barbecue business. Part of the fourth genera-tion—Charles's two sons, Chuck and Chris—

now help their father run the operation from the kitchen behind the busy takeout counter, while Charles's wife Ellen and daughter Carey pitch in when they're needed.

It's ironic that some die-hard natives of west Burlington have never given Hursey's a try, continuing to bypass his relatively new restaurant in favor of an older joint on the edge of town. There, they dine on electrically cooked barbecue and thick, pinkish coleslaw (made with mayonnaise and catsup), missing out on one of only a handful of North Carolina restaurants east of Greensboro where barbecue is slow cooked over real hardwood coals. But Hursey's continues to build on a solid reputation for both excellent restaurant fare and quality catering, and the place is normally packed at peak periods, particularly at lunchtime. Meanwhile, the wholesale business, located in a facility just north of Burlington, continues to prosper, keeping alive a tradition begun in 1949, when Charles's mother Daisy obtained the first barbecue wholesaler's license granted in North Carolina.

Charles Hursey says the family tradition began when his grandfather started to cook hogs out in his backyard as a hobby. Hursey's father, Sylvester, learned the basic technique as a child, but the business didn't really get started until Sylvester Hursey was a full-grown adult. Charles Hursey, a sober, churchgoing man, whose children all graduated from Alamance Christian School, tells the story— a little sheepishly—this way:

"When my Daddy was in his thirties or so, he was in his backyard with some friends, and they was drinkin' a little bit, so they decided to cook some hogs. Well, people were wanting to buy the meat and they sold all of it, in advance, before those hogs were even done. So he said, 'If I can do that drinkin', I know I can do it sober.'"

Sylvester built a little tin building in the backyard, maybe fourteen feet by eighteen feet; put up a swing nearby so the parents could keep an eye on Charles and his younger brother, Larry; and started cooking one hog per week. During this time, Sylvester Hursey was using a sauce recipe he got from his father, but one night, according to Charles, Sylvester won the recipe for a competitor's sauce in a poker game. Sylvester decided to combine the two recipes, thus creating the Hursey's sauce that is still used today.

It wasn't long before the business outgrew the backyard pit, so the Hurseys bought a little café in the small town of Gibsonville, near Burlington, and built two barbecue pits in the back to handle the growing volume. In addition to the café trade, the Hursey's built a sizable wholesale business, with Daisy Hursey using a station wagon to make deliveries all over the region.

**Larry and Charles Hursey outside their parents' original
barbecue pit in Gibsonville.**
Courtesy Charles Hursey

Charles began learning the business by helping his parents after school and during the summer. As soon as he graduated from high school in 1960, he plunged full-time into the family enterprise, quickly taking over the operation of the Gibsonville restaurant and the wholesale business at the same time. In 1966, he took over the operation of the takeout barbecue counter in Burlington that his father had opened several years earlier, and his brother, Larry, joined him in the family business. Today, Charles and Larry are partners in the wholesale side of the business, with Larry's son, Kent, serving as general manager.

In 1960, one of Charles Hursey's first acts as manager of the Gibsonville café was to welcome blacks through the front door as regular customers. At that time, most similar restaurants were still following Jim Crow customs that required African-Americans to place takeout orders around back. Later, when he took over the Burlington takeout stand, which was located in a predominately black neighborhood, his reputation for equal treatment preceded him, and his place was one of only a few spots in town where black and white customers regularly rubbed elbows. When ugly racial incidents broke out at nearby Williams High School in the late '60s, the unrest spread—and one evening a virtual riot occurred in the area all around Hursey's bar-becue counter. The next morning when Charles returned to work, nearly every store in the neighborhood had been vandalized, with many windows smashed, but his place was not touched. He later heard that the word had been passed among the rioters to spare Hursey's Barbecue, possibly so that the neighborhood residents would have someplace to eat the next day. Today, Hursey is proud of this legacy of equality. "We treated everybody fair and right, like it's supposed to be," he says.

Although his father and grandfather cooked whole hogs in the early days, Hursey follows the prevailing piedmont custom and roasts pork shoulders. The restaurant menu offers both chopped and what Hursey calls "pig pickin'" barbecue—hunks of meat that have been either sliced or pulled by hand from the shoulder. The regular barbecue is just a little too finely chopped for my particular taste—although a lot of customers prefer it that way. However, the "pig pickin'" meat has a substantial texture that invites a real bite, as well as being extremely tender and full of flavor.

The sauce is a mild but interesting blend between the hot vinegar of the east and the sugar-and-tomato-added sauces popular around Lexington. This isn't surprising considering Burlington's geographic location almost on the dividing line between the two barbecue styles. The sauce has achieved a loyal following. Hursey tells the anecdote of a young fellow from Burlington who accepted a job with a company in Japan and was invited to dinner one evening by his boss, a Japanese businessman. The evening progressed smoothly, and the boss eventually leaned across the table and murmured that he was getting ready to bring out something he unveiled only on very special occasions. Expecting some sort of wine or liqueur, the young man was flabbergasted to see the businessman reverently bring forth a bottle of Hursey's Barbecue Sauce—made right in the employee's North Carolina hometown.

Between the meat that came off his grill and the sauce that went on it, Hursey's obviously came up with the right taste combination to be judged the winner of the 1984 North-South Carolina Barbecue Bowl competition held in Washington, D.C. But the restaurant's biggest claim to fame has come from serving barbecue to Bill Clinton, George Bush, and Ronald Reagan. The barbecue that went to President Clinton and President Reagan was delivered by presidential staffers, who considered their own meals at Hursey's so good that they wanted to take some barbecue back to their boss in Washington. President Bush ate his Hursey's barbecue during the 1992 campaign. While Bush was in Burlington for a campaign stop, Hursey delivered a large order of barbecue directly to the president's train. After the secret service gave the box of barbecue and fixings the once-over, it was loaded on the train. Hursey later heard that the president was enjoying his barbecue before the train even reached Raleigh.

In addition to hardwood-cooked pork, the restaurant is also known around the area for what it calls "broasted" chicken, which is really fried chicken cooked in some sort of a pressure cooker that's supposed to keep it from getting excessively greasy. Now I firmly believe that fried chicken should ordinarily be cooked in a heavy skillet, but I can certainly attest, in the most complimentary way possible, that this chicken tastes pleasantly greasy, just the way wonderful fried chicken is supposed to taste. My wife and I have agreed after several tailgate gatherings that it's our favorite takeout chicken.

While other barbecue places are generally known for their fruit cobblers or banana pudding, Hursey's serves a firm, nicely browned, well-seasoned fried apple turnover. Quite a few people pull through Hursey's "pig up" window just for a sack of the warm, fried pies.

Whether you're in the mood for a fried pie or a full meal, you can easily reach Hursey's from Interstate 85/40 by taking the exit for N.C. 62. Follow N.C. 62 (also called Alamance Road) north to its intersection with

U.S. 70 (South Church Street), where you'll find Hursey's on the left. The restaurant is closed Sundays.

Stamey's Barbecue
Greensboro

I moved to Greensboro in 1972 as a young television reporter for WFMY-TV, and one of my most vivid recollections from my early days there is of Steve Campbell, our autocratic, five-foot-three-inch assignment editor, sitting at his U-shaped work station and barking orders into the mobile radio microphone. One day around noon, Steve had just dispatched one news crew to an accident he had picked up on the police scanner and had instructed another to head toward one of the high schools to check out reports of a large fight. A call came in from a hungry news photographer saying he had finished a shooting assignment and wanted to take his lunch break. Steve loved to use police lingo, so he grabbed the microphone and asked the fellow's "10-20," or location. When he found that the news car was eastbound on High Point Road, near the coliseum, he barked, "Pull into the drive-through at Stamey's, get two barbecue sandwiches, and head straight

downtown to cover the city council meeting." No protest ever came back over the squawky radio receiver, so I suppose the cameraman—probably just as green as I was—meekly followed instructions.

There were some things you just didn't argue about in those days, and Stamey's reputation for having the best barbecue in Greensboro was one of them. At that time, the rambling, white-frame restaurant sitting across from the Greensboro Coliseum was the end result of several remodelings and additions made since the original drive-in opened in 1953. Traffic on High Point Road wasn't as heavy twenty-five years ago, and crowds from the Big Four and ACC basketball tournaments used to line the boulevard, waiting for breaks between oncoming cars so they could dash across the avenue to dine at Stamey's between games. Occasionally, newspaper and television reporters and photographers from around the Triad used to share a table at the restaurant, and I can clearly remember sipping ice tea and listening to a young New York native rejoice about having landed a reporting job back in North Carolina, where he had attended college. "Man, I've eaten barbecue and hush puppies here every day since I got back," he exclaimed proudly.

Today, Stamey's occupies a newer building, constructed on the same site in the '80s, and it's fitting that its quarters are probably the most impressive among all the barbecue restaurants in North Carolina. Stamey's is, after all, one of the proudest names in the business, and as I've recounted elsewhere in this book, its founder, Warner Stamey, taught the secrets of the barbecue craft to the operators of some of the piedmont's best-known barbecue establishments. A portrait of Warner Stamey hangs just inside the front door of the restaurant. Not far from Stamey's portrait are two smaller, black-and-white pictures that present a fascinating contrast with the polished brass, brick, and wood of the cathedral-ceilinged building. The aging photographs show the emporiums of the two men who popularized Lexington-style barbecue and taught the process of its preparation to Warner Stamey. One picture shows a semipermanent tent set up as a barbecue stand in the '20s by Jess Swicegood, while the other reveals a tiny cafe built a few years later by Sid Weaver—who had originally set up a barbecue tent right beside Swicegood's just a few yards from the county courthouse in Lexington. From these humble beginnings grew dozens of restaurants all across piedmont North Carolina—all serving the same slow-roasted, chopped pork shoulders and tangy-sweet, vinegar-and-tomato sauce that were perfected by Swicegood and Weaver, and passed along through Warner Stamey.

The real monument to Stamey is not the restaurant but the pit building, which is by far the largest and best equipped in the state. Warner was constantly experimenting with the design of the wood-fired pits used to cook pork shoulders. While the pits pictured in early photographs were essentially open-top, rectangular boxes with metal covers that could be raised and shut, the ten pits at Stamey's are basically a series of large brick ovens forming a solid wall along each side of the rectangular building. Fireplaces for burning wood down to coals are also built into the walls. The wood is thrown into the fireplaces through an exterior door beside the woodpile, while coals are shoveled from doors inside the building and into the pits. Each pit has two sets of steel doors, one providing access to the metal cooking racks, the other to the floors of the pits where the hickory coals are spread, twenty-four inches below the roasting shoulders. Smoke from the pits is vented outside through chimneys, rather than emerging directly into the pit building as it does at several establishments. With its dull red brick, arched fireplaces, and black steel doors, the place has the look and feel of a nineteenth-century foundry . . . a look of permanence and solidity perfectly matched to the reputation of Warner Stamey.

Lockey Reynolds, a lean, wizened man in his sixties, has presided over the pits for many years, drawing coals from the fireplaces with a long-handled shovel and scattering them evenly beneath the meat, and, when the time

NORTH CAROLINA BARBECUE : *Flavored by Time*

is right, bending from the waist and leaning into the smoky pits to turn the heavy shoulders with a three-foot fork.

Keith and Charles Stamey, Warner's sons, have run the restaurant for nearly thirty years, and Charles's son, Chip, is now helping manage the operation. Keith, the restaurant's unofficial spokesperson and the more visible of the two brothers, left a ten-year military career and joined his brother in the business in 1970, three years after Warner Stamey passed along its ownership. The restaurant is a large, cheerful, bustling place that's always crowded at peak periods, and a second location on the north side of town also does a thriving business. (The barbecue is all cooked on the pits at the main restaurant and then trucked to the satellite location.)

The tender, smoky pork is served up chopped or sliced, although "sliced" in most piedmont barbecue places—including this one—means broken up into appetizing, juicy pieces rather than cleanly sliced like ham or rare roast beef. Due to the heavy volume at Stamey's, the chopped barbecue is cut by machine, and the only minor complaint I might have is that this implement gets it a little too finely chopped for my personal taste. The overall texture, flavor, and tenderness are superb, nonetheless.

Stamey's sauce seems to be just a bit sweeter than most other Lexington-style sauces. It is not thick at all, and when a small amount is ladled over a serving of chopped barbecue, the liquid seeps down and moistens the meat from top to bottom, rather than resting atop the barbecue like catsup or a commercially thick barbecue sauce.

Since my family comes from eastern North Carolina, nearly all the barbecue and fixings I ate during my childhood and adolescence came from that region of the state. When I moved to Greensboro, the piedmont-style barbecue meal served by Stamey's looked decidedly odd to me, with strange, reddish green coleslaw and thin, crescent-shaped hush puppies that were far different from the balls of fried corn bread I had heretofore encountered. However, I quickly grew to love Stamey's hush puppies, which are sweet and light and don't fill you up while you're waiting for your barbecue to arrive. I later found out that Stamey's uses a head on its hush puppy machine that was originally designed to form miniature doughnuts; it's been modified so that it cuts the cornmeal "doughnuts" in half as they drop into the deep fryer.

Stamey's unquestionably serves the tangiest coleslaw in North Carolina. The cabbage is chopped into fine bits about the size of air rifle pellets and dressed with a peppery sweet-and-sour sauce that has considerably more kick than the barbecue sauce. The mild, sweet coleslaw of the east may serve to soothe the palate in between bites of tart, pepper-flavored barbecue, but at Stamey's, the slaw has a definite bite, waking up the naturally sweet, smoky flavored barbecue in the same way ground horseradish wakes up roast beef. I personally find Stamey's slaw to be a bracing accompaniment to the 'cue, but some first-timers find that it takes some getting used to. While every single customer may not like this side dish, no one ever forgets it.

No one ever forgets the fruit cobbler at Stamey's, either, but you would be hard-pressed to find a complaint about this dish among the customers. Keith Stamey is downright fussy about the restaurant's peach cobbler, which he says outsells the apple and cherry versions by about ten to one. When I was invited to discuss North Carolina barbecue as a guest on ABC's *Good Morning, America*, I asked Keith Stamey to make a peach cobbler that I could add to the table full of barbecue, hush puppies, coleslaw, and other dishes I was getting together for the segment. He actually made four cobblers before he ended up with one that he thought looked good enough for national television; the others cooked over and had juice running down the sides of the dish, which to me is exactly the way they're supposed to look. Ironically, Keith's perfect cobbler looked great on the air, but time constraints kept me from even getting to mention it on that occasion. Now, however, I finally feel that I've done it justice.

A 1996 poll published in *The State* magazine named Stamey's as one of North Carolina's two best barbecue restaurants. Personally, I'd have a great deal of trouble narrowing my choices down to two, but there's no question that Stamey's is right up there at the top. Whenever I'm on the west side of Greensboro, I enjoy simply riding by the place—watching the smoke billow from the pits and breathing in the enchanting aroma that spreads for blocks around.

The simplest way to reach Stamey's from any direction in Greensboro is to follow signs for the Greensboro Coliseum, since the restaurant is almost directly opposite the coliseum on High Point Road. From Interstate 40, proceed north on High Point Road; Stamey's will be on the left. Closed Sunday.

Short Sugar's Drive-In
Reidsville

Of all the barbecue restaurants in America, Short Sugar's Drive-In has to have the greatest name. Johnny, Clyde, and Eldridge Overby had planned to call their new business the Overby Brothers Drive-In. But two days before it was to open in June 1949, Eldridge Overby was killed in an auto accident. Instead of using the original name, Johnny and Clyde decided to honor their brother, who had been known as "Short Sugar," by naming the place after him alone. Now, as to why Eldridge had that particular nickname, the stories vary. It seems well established that he was short, which takes care of the first half. But as for "Sugar," time has muddled people's recollections of whether it was because Eldridge was exceptionally friendly, with an attractive laugh, or whether it was because the ladies considered him kind of cute. In any case, even though Eldridge didn't live to see the restaurant open, his nickname has certainly been immortalized, since it's the one thing no one ever forgets about the place.

Today, Short Sugar's sits at the same location, and it still looks like a '50s-style teenage hangout, which is exactly what it became on the first day it was open. There are even drive-in parking spaces where you still can get curb service just by tooting your horn. And although Short Sugar's may not be a hot gathering spot for the current students of Reidsville High School, the folks who grew up in town during the '50s, '60s, and '70s still flock to the place, along with seekers from all over central North Carolina who have heard about the barbecue and had their interest piqued by the name.

As a reporter for WFMY-TV in Greensboro during the '70s, I was assigned to cover Rockingham County for awhile, which meant that I made frequent lunch stops at both Short Sugar's in Reidsville and Fuzzy's in Madison—the two spots anyone would tell you had the best barbecue in the northern piedmont. Part of the job of covering this

largely rural county involved keeping up with the local daily and weekly newspapers, and I would sometimes spend part of a slow day sitting in Short Sugar's reading the *Reidsville Review* and listening for local gossip that might develop into a story.

Reidsville was always a tobacco center—the place where unfiltered Lucky Strike cigarettes were manufactured at the big American Tobacco Company factory in the middle of town for more than fifty years. The town's minor league baseball team during the '40s and '50s was even called the Reidsville Luckies, and fans used to marvel over the exploits of players from the team like home-run slugger Leo "Muscle" Shoals as they enjoyed their barbecue sandwiches at Short Sugar's. Now, both the team and the company that inspired their name are gone. American Tobacco's long decline and periodic downsizing have been an immense blow to Reidsville, since the corporation had long been the town's leading employer (it's now been taken over by Brown & Williamson). While Reidsville is struggling to stay afloat and diversify its economic base, it's sobering to think how the community's spirits might sag to a critical point if anything ever happened to Short Sugar's.

But at a time when the world seems to be shifting beneath their feet, it must be comforting for Reidsville natives to grab a stool at Short Sugar's counter and see veterans Bill and Louise Whaley at work, just as they have been for nearly forty years. Louise comes in at 3:30 A.M., six days a week, to make biscuits and cook bacon, sausage, and grits for breakfast, while Bill is the one who knows more than anyone else about how the barbecue ought to be prepared. Short Sugar's only chops or slices what pork it needs at the moment so that the meat will taste fresh, and it's Bill's job to cut up the hams and shoulders and fill the orders as they arrive. He only works part-time now, but he trains high school students to chop barbecue, which bodes well for Short Sugar's future labor needs.

The restaurant pit-cooks its barbecue (hams for sliced, shoulders for chopped) over hickory coals in two small pits that are located near enough to the counter so that everyone can watch when it's time to turn the meat or spread more coals. The barbecue is served with a thin, dark sauce that's mixed up, according to the original recipe, by David Wilson, the son-in-law of one of the founders who now co-owns the restaurant with Kerry Key. Short Sugar's sauce, which Bill Whaley says is the key reason for the barbecue's reputation, seems to have less catsup or tomato paste than some of the popular piedmont "dips," and there's a definite presence of both sugar and Worcestershire sauce that adds a heated pungency to the mixture. The sauce and the meat obviously blended well on the judges' palates during the 1982 Barbecue Bowl cook-off between North and South Carolina, held in Washington, D.C., since Short Sugar's was the first restaurant from either state to be crowned champion. (In a maddening bit of political correctness, the inaugural event the previous year had been declared a tie.)

While Short Sugar's is justly famous for both its sliced and chopped barbecue—both of which are lean, tender, and smoky tasting—I can't quite understand the community's taste for "minced" barbecue. This is pork that's chopped ultrafine and served swimming in sauce—a sort of barbecue chili, if you will. The only other place where I've encountered minced barbecue is Bridges Barbecue Lodge in Shelby, and I can't say I really enjoyed pork served in this form at either place. Now, if you're a local who has grown fond of this particular specialty—well, God bless—but if you aren't already hooked, I'd suggest you enjoy Short Sugar's notable barbecue in its most delicious and appetizing form, which is either chopped or sliced.

Reidsville is north of Greensboro, off of U.S. 29. From the south, take U.S. 29 Business into Reidsville and bear right on Scales Street; Short Sugar's will be on the left. From the north, exit from U.S. 29 onto N.C. 87 North and follow this highway into Reidsville, then turn south onto Scales Street; travel several blocks and you'll see the restaurant on the right. Closed Sunday.

NORTH CAROLINA BARBECUE : *Flavored by Time*

Fuzzy's
Madison

Fuzzy's has been serving authentic, hickory-cooked barbecue since 1954, when it was opened by T.H. "Fuzzy" Nelson. Because of its somewhat out-of-the-way location in Madison, some twenty-five miles north of Greensboro, it hasn't developed the statewide reputation enjoyed by some of North Carolina's other barbecue restaurants, but it has been a household name to barbecue lovers from the Triad area and the northern piedmont, including those in the town of Eden, where Fuzzy's has had a satellite location operating for a number of years. Coincidentally, two fairly well-publicized attempts to market North Carolina barbecue in New York City both happened to involve Fuzzy's. Neither venture was successful, but the restaurant never missed a beat among its fans in the local area, and it continues to be very much a part of the ebb and flow of ordinary life in western Rockingham County.

"Barbecue in *New York City*?," you can almost hear North Carolinians snarl. Well, it seems that New York talk-radio host Barry Farber, a native of Greensboro, got the idea back in 1977 that North Carolina barbecue would sweep New Yorkers off their feet if there were only a way to properly introduce them to the delicacy. Obviously, pit-cooking the pork in the middle of Manhattan was out of the question, so the next best thing would be to find a supplier in North Carolina who would prepare the barbecue, then ship it overnight to New York. Farber remembered Fuzzy's from his Greensboro days, and he talked a friend who owned a Times Square building into flying down for a taste test. The friend fell hard for the barbecue, and the would-be importers found that Fuzzy's had an existing wholesale branch that could easily handle the preparation and shipment. The problem was that the friend's ground-floor space on Times Square was leased to a proprietor selling Greek specialties and bagels. The building owner basically coerced his tenant, who was behind on his rent, into adding the North Carolina barbecue to his menu. However, the reluctant restaurateur was apparently content to serve the alien chopped pork on cold buns, often with no coleslaw, and outraged Tar Heels living in New York complained that the place was giving North Carolina barbecue a bad name. The last straw was added, and the experiment came to an abrupt end, when Farber took a friend by for a sandwich and the two were served barbecue—pork barbecue—on a bagel.

Ten years later, veteran magazine and television model Zacki Murphy, a Hillsborough native and unabashed barbecue lover, hired vendors to sell North Carolina barbecue sandwiches from a pushcart on Fifth Avenue, occasionally donning suspended overalls to fill in personally for the cart operators between modeling assignments. Like Farber, Zacki arranged for Fuzzy's wholesale operation to cook the barbecue over an open pit, but the chopped pork was then mixed with her own special Lexington-style sauce before it was fast-frozen for shipment to New York. The vending cart operation was short-lived, and although Murphy later tried selling her trademark barbecue from a small, storefront-type restaurant, the venture was plagued by constant problems with unreliable help and high overhead.

It may be that a barbecue place, with its unhurried pace and atmosphere of conviviality and trust, just isn't suited for the mean streets of a place like New York, but through the years, Fuzzy's seems to have done just fine back home in Madison. The interior of the restaurant has recently been remodeled, adding some warmer wood tones to the decor, but the restaurant basically remains unchanged: the outside of the restaurant still looks much as it has for the past thirty years or so, the same curb service is available, local businessmen in suits still crowd the counter at lunchtime, and the pork hams and shoulders are still cooked for long hours over hickory wood. Sheriff's deputies and highway patrol troopers who have eaten regularly at Fuzzy's for a quarter-century still occupy their favorite booths and stools several days each week. One of these officers told me with a straight face that if a felon in custody begged for a last meal at Fuzzy's, he'd bring the miscreant in for one final sandwich before carting him off to jail.

Chopped barbecue is prepared from shoulders at Fuzzy's, but the whiter meat from pork hams is preferred for sliced barbecue, which is fairly popular in these parts. The chopped barbecue is cut very fine, the way you'd expect to find it in the eastern half of the state. But the similarity ends there, because unlike its eastern cousin, Fuzzy's chopped barbecue is as heavily moistened by sauce as any I've encountered in North Carolina. The sauce, which has always been considered the real secret to the barbecue at Fuzzy's, is a mild and fairly sweet Lexington-style blend, with tomato catsup added to a vinegar base. Now if I were mixing up the barbecue, I might not stir in quite as much sauce as does Dickie Kellam, who's been doing the cooking at Fuzzy's for fifteen years, but he and veteran manager Ricky Bullins certainly know their customers' tastes better than I do. Ah, well . . . I believe this moist barbecue would go better on a nice, soft bun, topped with some of Fuzzy's tart, peppery coleslaw, than in a plain barbecue tray, which is what I ordered on my last visit. Next time I'll order a sandwich and just enjoy the extra sauce as a special, local touch. When in Rome . . .

You'll enjoy the fresh-tasting hush puppies at Fuzzy's, or perhaps I should say the hush *puppy*. As it has been for years, the batter is squeezed by hand from a pastry bag into the hot cooking oil in one long swirl, so that you end up with a single, serpentine coil of fried corn bread, which you can make into as many hush puppies as you like. The mix contains tasty bits of onion, but the pups still taste straightforwardly of cornmeal and are not overly sweet.

If you visit Fuzzy's on a Wednesday, you'll more than likely find the place packed to the rafters, with a bowl of pinto beans sitting in front of virtually every customer. The beans, as you might imagine, are perfectly seasoned with pork—what else—and the kitchen staff swears that they just can't cook enough to feed everyone who wants some.

A final note: Be sure to try the banana pudding, which comes with a rich, golden meringue topping.

Fuzzy's is located on Business U.S. 220 in Madison. From the south, exit the U.S. 220 Bypass onto U.S. 311 and follow it into Madison, then turn north onto Business U.S. 220. From the north, exit off the bypass directly onto Business U.S. 220 and follow it towards Madison until you reach the restaurant. Open daily.

The Barbecue Trail
Salisbury to Albemarle

OK, it's a little off the beaten track for most people, but in my judgment, the twenty-five mile stretch of U.S. 52 between Salisbury and Albemarle, in Rowan and Stanly Counties, is one of the richest veins of tasty, piedmont-style barbecue I've ever prospected. All of the outstanding places along this stretch are small, and none have far-reaching reputations, but they all serve a superior barbecue sandwich, which is the only item I sampled at each place. These spots are all located directly on U.S. 52, leading my UNC-TV camera crewmen, Jerome Moore and Scott Scherr, to christen this part of the highway as "The Barbecue Trail."

Located in Granite Quarry, just south of Salisbury, **M & K Barbecue and Country Cookin'** is a fairly new place, opened in an existing restaurant building in 1990 by Moran and Kathy Thomas. Someone apparently used to do some big-time barbecuing at this location since there are enough unused pits around back to cook about four hundred shoulders at once, but Moran just barbecues a few shoulders each day in a smaller pit up front. He does it right, though, over real wood coals, taking the same care with his barbecue that he does with menu items such as country-style steak—made the slow, time-consuming way. Moran's father spent quite a few years cooking barbecue, but Moran got into the business when he decided to get off the road after some twenty-five years as a truck driver, which may explain his fondness for the country-style items on his menu. Your barbecue sandwich at M&K will be thick with moist, tender chunks of reddish brown, smoke-flavored pork; enlivened by a splash of tangy sauce; and topped by coarse, red, piedmont-style slaw. Closed Sunday and Monday.

Some five miles down the road, in Rockwell, there's a well-known old landmark known as **Darrell's**. The restaurant is still named after the previous owner, Darrell Galloway, although he recently sold out to Dick and Pat Arey. The building is a tiny yellow bungalow with a steeply pitched roof, resembling an oversized playhouse, and it was reportedly known far and wide as a popular teen gathering spot as far back as the early '40s. When I stopped by, before the change in ownership, the interior decor was colorful and the barbecue sandwich was superb, with a definite taste of wood smoke. The new owners say the restaurant is selling more barbecue since they bought the place, and they've added some new items, such as a rib-eye steak plate. Seafood is also a popular menu selection. Open Wednesday through Saturday.

As you approach the outskirts of Albemarle,

you will come across **Log Cabin Barbecue**, which is housed, as you might expect from the name, in a rustic log building. However, the most important logs at this place are the lengths of hickory piled up out back beside the barbecue pits, which let you know right away that some serious pit cooking goes on here. Owner Glen Almond, a hardworking man who seldom stands still, has had the place for six or seven years, and he personally fires the pits and tends to the cooking when he isn't busy filling drive-up orders at the restaurant's back door. The barbecue at Log Cabin is deeply flavored by hickory smoke, and the sandwiches are topped with a delicious, unusual coleslaw that almost has a bit of a "pickled" taste. Closed Sunday.

A mile or so down the road toward downtown Albemarle is **Whispering Pines Barbecue**, housed in another quaint, diminutive bungalow fronted by a colorful, '50s-style sign in the shape of a towering pine tree. Begun in 1945 by Lonnie Doby, Whispering Pines has been owned and operated in recent years by his widow, Lavada Doby. Lavada is a friendly, talkative woman who admits she probably should have expanded the seating capacity beyond the current twenty-to-twenty-five at some point, but, she says, "I was always just too busy." Whispering Pines still turns out genuine, hickory-cooked barbecue, seasoned with a sauce that's much closer to an eastern North Carolina mixture

NORTH CAROLINA BARBECUE : *Flavored by Time*

than to the Lexington-style dip you might expect in this area of the state. This place also has the unofficial distinction of serving what must be the most generous portions of barbecue in the entire state of North Carolina. Closed Sunday and Monday.

Barbecue Center
Lexington

If you're approaching Lexington from the direction of High Point or Greensboro, and you determine that you need barbecue *immediately*, Sonny Conrad's Barbecue Center is the answer to your prayers. Not only is it the first of twenty restaurants that you'll come to, it's one of the few places in town that still cooks entirely with wood; Sonny even has a printed handout he'll give you explaining exactly how the process is carried out. Sonny's ancestors came to this country from Germany, and a touch of Germanic thoroughness such as this proves that barbecue, like most everything else, benefits from ethnic diversity. Because of Barbecue Center's authenticity, its efficiency, and most of all, its favorable location within a stone's throw of the main Lexington exit, I feel entirely justified in naming it an official "Emergency Barbecue Treat-

ment Center" and conferring upon it all the privileges of that title.

Most of the time, the cooking at Barbecue Center is done on a couple of pits built onto the kitchen, but on special occasions, like the day before the annual Lexington Barbecue Festival, the restaurant's older, outside pits are fired up. Even these "special" pits have now been enclosed in a metal shed, but the shelter's doors are usually thrown open so that the smoke rolls out across the parking lot and onto North Main Street, reminding everyone on that end of town of what lies in store when the festival kicks off the next day. The festival's several sponsoring restaurants, including Barbecue Center, cook some twelve thousand pounds of extra barbecue between them, which is sold at a furious pace in three large tents on the courthouse square. That's not counting the large amount of meat that has to be cooked for each individual restaurant, since festival day brings every place in town its biggest volume of the year.

The media coverage for the Lexington Barbecue Festival is intense, and Sonny's place is usually the spot where TV folks, including crews from the national shows, go to do their stories on advance preparations for the festival, since it's the easiest location in which to shoot without having to traipse through the kitchen and get under everyone's feet. Locals also drop by during this day of preparation; the entire time the meat's on the fire there's usually a knot of observers standing with their hands in their pockets, sniffing the incomparable aroma of pork roasting over wood coals and hoping to be offered a crunchy nibble pulled from the outside of one of the shoulders.

Conrad came by his barbecue skill honestly. One of his grandfathers used to cook shoulders on a backyard pit every Friday during the mid 1940s, while the other grandfather, a tobacco farmer, was known for cooking chickens over a pit. "We always ate big at corn shuckings and tobacco curings," remembers Conrad. However, it was through his wife's family that he happened to go into the barbecue business himself. His brother-in-law, who at one time worked for Warner Stamey, used to operate a dairy bar and barbecue restaurant further up Main Street, and in 1961, he built what is now Barbecue Center. When Sonny got out of the service in the early '60s, he came back and worked with his brother-in-law, and when the relative died in 1967, Conrad bought the place. Today, Barbecue Center is still a family affair, in keeping with North Carolina tradition. His wife Nancy and his sister, Betty Ruth, help him run the restaurant, while his son, Michael, presently is working full-time and another son, Cecil, pitches in when he's needed.

Like so many barbecue spots, this one was built as a drive-in, and the original shelter is still in place over the parking spots where curb service was once available. Although there are no longer any carhops, there's still a little drive-in ambiance, since Sonny's is one of the few places around town where you can get a genuine, hand-dipped banana split, the kind that takes about fifteen minutes to make. There's a big neon sign advertising this specialty, and families bring their kids in, especially in the summertime, to be entertained by the girls who make the desserts.

As for the barbecue, it's good, solid, genuine stuff, coming straight from the heart of the Lexington tradition and cooked for nine hours or more over glowing hickory coals. Served chopped and sliced, the meat is tender and naturally sweet, and the standard red slaw and hush puppies set it off to perfection. Barbecue Center isn't one of Lexington's largest restaurants, but as Conrad is quick to point out, "This is one town where the little boys aren't automatically eaten up by the big boys the way they are other places."

Barbecue Center is located in Lexington at 900 North Main Street. From the I-85 Business loop, also known as U.S. 29/70, follow the signs for downtown Lexington, which will lead you directly onto Main Street. If you're approaching from the north, you'll see the restaurant almost immediately on your right. Closed Sunday.

Jimmy's Barbecue
Lexington

The popularity of barbecue grew out of our need to celebrate something—a special event such as a commencement, perhaps, or maybe the successful completion of a lengthy process, such as the harvesting of crops. But as you look at those barbecue restaurants that have been most successful over the years, you'll find that something else has been celebrated there as well: family togetherness. It just seems that a barbecue restaurant was meant to be run by a family and handed down from one generation to the next. When the owner of a successful place sells out or appears to lose interest, it's often because he or she has no family member coming along who's interested in keeping the business going. In most cases, however, there is someone in the family who wants to keep the tradition alive. It's amazing, really, how many children who grow up helping their parents operate a barbecue restaurant end up going into the business themselves, even after going to college and exploring other career options. There's obviously a deep satisfaction in serving good food to people, even when it requires sharing a lot of hard, dirty, unglamorous work and many long, inconvenient hours. Restaurant work, particularly cooking barbecue, has been categorized among the world's most demanding jobs, but members of barbecue families speak more often about the fulfilling sense of continuity they find in preparing food the same way every day, or the satisfaction to be derived from constantly trying to improve service and quality, than the hardships involved.

If you want to see a barbecue family portrait in the flesh, stop by Jimmy's Barbecue in Lexington. You'll find owner Jimmy Harvey; his wife Betty; two sons, Terry (the manager) and Kemp; and two daughters, Kirskey and Karen, working in the restaurant fulltime, while six of Harvey's eight grandchildren also work at Jimmy's from time to time if needed. Even when they aren't working, which is seldom, members of this family often vacation together at the beach or at nearby High Rock Lake. With all the pressures that tend to drive families apart today, I'm convinced Jimmy Harvey and his family know something that a lot of the rest of us don't know. Maybe it would be worth a trip to Jimmy's just to ask them what it is, or go simply for the pleasure of observing a family that works hard and sticks together.

Incidentally, the barbecue is pretty darn good at Jimmy's, too. Harvey ought to know what he's doing by now, since he's been at it for nearly fifty-five years. Like some other pretty well-known barbecuers around Lexington, he started out working part-time, then full-time, for Warner Stamey, and during those early years, he also had a chance to work with another barbecue pioneer, Sid Weaver. When he opened his own place in Thomasville in 1958, he already had sixteen years experience in the barbecue business, and by the time Jimmy's opened at its present Lexington location in 1970, he'd been cooking pork shoulders, with all the trimmings, for twenty-eight years.

Jimmy's serves true, Lexington-style, pork-shoulder barbecue, cooked long and slow, chopped by hand, and seasoned with a sauce that, even in its milder version, may be the hottest in town. The 'cue isn't chopped superfine but has an appealing chunky texture. Outside brown meat is available by special order, either chopped or sliced. Since the "brown" typically has a stronger smoke flavor and more toothsome texture than any other part of the shoulder, I'd recommend that you be sure to try this treat, which you'll generally only find at a handful of Lexington restaurants.

Harvey told me his barbecue is still cooked entirely over wood coals "because smoke is one of the best advertisements in the world. People can smell it all the way out on the highway." In Jimmy's case, that's saying a lot, since his restaurant is located at least two hundred yards off Interstate 85. But he's convinced that motorists often catch a whiff of smoke from his pits in time to make the exit for N.C. 8 and pull into his place for a sand-wich, even when they hadn't planned to stop.

Jimmy's regular sauce has more red and black pepper and less sweetener than the typical Lexington sauces you'll find at other spots around town. His so-called "hot, hot" dip is even more invigorating, although it's certainly nothing to be intimidated about, especially when compared to a full-bore eastern sauce like that found at Scott's or Wilber's. Jimmy's sauce is thicker than either of those sauces, though, and you'll probably have to stir it around a little bit after you put it on the barbecue in order to get the full effect.

Around Lexington, Jimmy's may be just about as well known for its barbecued chicken as for its pork barbecue. Harvey cooks chicken Thursday through Sunday only, but on those days you can just about bet that every one of his 125 seats will be full, at least during peak hours. The half-chickens are slowly grilled for hours until they're a deep, rich brown, then brushed with just enough sauce to soften the good, crispy skin just a bit. The chicken is moist and tender, with a wonderful light smoky flavor.

Harvey, a gentle, genial man with eyes crinkled by years of smiling, grows serious when he talks about the future of pit-cooked barbecue around Lexington. He believes events like the annual Lexington Barbecue Festival, for which Jimmy's is one of the sponsoring restaurants, will continue to help maintain a certain market for the regional specialty,

NORTH CAROLINA BARBECUE : *Flavored by Time*

but he thinks a combination of rising costs, environmental regulations, and changing tastes will cut down on the number of places willing to go to the trouble to cook with wood. "There's a shortage of people who will even bring you wood, and when you can get it, it's tripled in price from what it used to be," he points out. "The folks with wood can make more money having it chipped up for sale as landscaping mulch."

Say it ain't so, Jimmy. And hang in there as long as you can.

Jimmy's is located just off the I-85 Business loop in Lexington. Take Exit 91 (the Southmont exit) and turn south on N.C. 8; you'll see Jimmy's on the immediate right. Closed Tuesday.

Lexington Barbecue
Lexington

The highway that passes within fifty yards of Lexington Barbecue's front door used to be a part of Interstate 85 between Greensboro and Charlotte. However, several years ago, I-85 was relocated so that it now bypasses Lexington several miles to the east. The former route now mostly carries local traffic along the furniture corridor stretching from High Point through Thomasville to Lexing-

ton. But owner Wayne Monk never lost a dollar's worth of business when the interstate was moved . . . because to the faithful, *all* roads still lead to Lexington Barbecue. Today, Monk is not only the undisputed barbecue chief of Lexington (a town with twenty barbecue places), he's also become perhaps the most widely known of all North Carolina's barbecue restaurateurs.

There are several very good barbecue restaurants in Lexington, but none serve the town's famous, wood-smoked pork shoulder in a more lean, moist, and tender, yet firmly textured, state than does Wayne Monk. The restaurant itself is bright and clean but unremarkable, and the side dishes, while perfectly rendered, are few. The meat is the thing here—enhanced to perfection by a dark, rather thin sauce or "dip" that is neither too mild nor too fiery. The meat's reputation is reflected in the restaurant's unusual clientele: while all of Lexington's barbecue restaurants seem to get their fair share of trade from local customers—who tend to stick with one favorite place—Lexington Barbecue attracts a large share of barbecue pilgrims from all across the state, and even some from further abroad. These are people who have left the interstate and driven several miles out of their way to reach this mecca, and they usually emerge from their cars with a gleam of purposefulness in their eye and move toward the restaurant with steps quickened by anticipation.

Many of them have been here before, and it's the meat that has brought them back.

A fortuitous series of circumstances has helped Monk achieve his current position, but he'll tell you that the real luck came in the fact that he was a natural hard worker and that he chose the right man to imitate. In Warner Stamey—a pioneer in establishing Lexington barbecue—Monk found a mentor who exuded both pride in the craft of barbecuing and a strong drive to achieve excellence. Today, Lexington Barbecue is one of at least three venerable barbecue places in the piedmont that owe their existence to Warner Stamey's ideas.

Monk got his first restaurant job as a sixteen-year-old carhop at a Lexington barbecue joint, but he says that at the time he was more interested in hot dogs and cheeseburgers, and didn't really understand what attracted people to barbecue. During the next ten years, Monk "bounced around a good bit," working a variety of jobs, but several of those years were spent working directly under Warner Stamey at his place in downtown Lexington. Monk began to absorb Stamey's vision of Lexington-style barbecue as a legitimate, distinctive regional specialty, and he gradually came to appreciate Stamey's talent for surrounding himself with good, reliable people who shared his enthusiasm for the product and its demanding method of preparation.

In 1962, with considerable experience under his belt for a man of twenty-six, Monk had a lucky opportunity to buy a prime roadside location beside U.S. 29/70, the same location his restaurant has occupied for the past thirty-three years. Ironically, both Stamey and Holland Tussey, another former boss, had owned the parcel of land previously, but neither had ever done anything with it. Monk, on the other hand, has not only made a go of it, he's added onto the place five times over the years.

Monk's early good fortune held: right after he opened the restaurant, it quickly became popular as a teenage hangout. However, it wasn't long before he began to realize that spending a lot of late-night hours with a restaurant full of high school kids was exhausting and not particularly profitable. With a fresh image in mind, Monk worked hard over the next several years to reposition the restaurant as a place catering to families and devoted to the slow, painstaking preparation of succulent meat—barbecue that would later have much of the state beating a path to his door.

Today, Lexington Barbecue is the kind of place that's not only warm and inviting, but also one where a first-time visitor is immediately put at ease by the helpful staff people, who are prepared to cheerfully and quickly explain the delightful variety of ways in which barbecue can be delivered to the table. The restaurant's mode of operation is very much a reflection of the personality and magnetism of Wayne Monk, who is an animated, outgoing man with a youthful, elfin face. He spends much of his time working the counter and cash register at the front of the restaurant, where he can chat and joke with customers, although he has begun rotating this duty among his son Rick and his two sons-in-law, all of whom normally work in the kitchen. (Monk's brother also works in the restaurant, his two daughters help out part-time, and he jokes that he's only able to hire about one person out of every hundred who apply because "there are so many cousins who want a job, too.")

While Monk is known as a man who looks out for his own and pays his employees well, he also demands a high level of performance. At peak periods, the kitchen looks a little like the bridge of a warship called to battle stations, with every position manned and every person alertly attending to his assigned details of food preparation and presentation. Waitresses, who tend to stay on for a long time once they're hired, must have, as Monk puts it, the "right appearance, attitude, and chemistry" to mix well with the families and older adults he wants to attract to the restaurant. Orders are quickly delivered to the tables, and tea glasses are kept full.

On the pits at the back of the restaurant, pork shoulders roast for ten hours over mostly oak coals, with hickory added when it's available. Veteran attendants shovel fresh coals from the fireboxes and scatter them under the dripping meat every thirty minutes or so, and they turn the shoulders so that the exposed meat side is facing up once it has roasted over the embers to a deep, dark brown.

Wayne Monk and his personally trained staff can take one of these beautifully browned, tender pork shoulders apart like the pieces of a puzzle. The skin lifts off in one piece and is discarded, and the excess fat is quickly trimmed. The outside "brown" is removed and set aside for special orders. Then the meat is pulled off the shoulder in large, pinkish brown chunks and placed on a chopping board until it's needed. As the orders come in, the succulent pork is either sliced, chopped into coarse chunks, or chopped more finely, then it is piled on a plate, a tray, or a sandwich bun. Sauce is ladled over the meat just before it leaves the kitchen so that the barbecue comes to the table moist but not saturated.

If you want a little foretaste of heaven, order a tray of the sliced "brown," the chewy outside meat that absorbs so much of the oak- or hickory-smoke flavor. While many barbecue places chop this portion of the shoulder into the other chopped meat, Monk's place serves it separately in order to satisfy all the customers who think, as I do, that it's absolutely the most delicious kind of meat on

Lexington Barbecue's Wayne Monk

earth. But you'll need to arrive early for lunch or dinner in order to be sure of getting some, since they usually run out of "brown" early in every meal service.

The coleslaw and the hush puppies at Lexington Barbecue are as good as you'll find anywhere, and I particularly noticed that the pups had a good, fresh cornmeal taste, with little hint of sweetness or onion. Frankly, though, the barbecue itself is so outstanding here that the side dishes subside into a purely complementary role.

Monk's barbecue is so good, it's even been served to world leaders. In 1983, Monk was asked by a politically connected local attor-

ney if he would be interested in preparing barbecue for President Reagan. Not thinking much about it, Monk answered in the affirmative. The next thing Monk knew, he was being booked by White House staffers to cater a meal for the heads of state of the world's seven leading industrial countries. A major economic summit meeting had been scheduled in Williamsburg, Virginia, and the president wanted to introduce his guests to genuine, American cuisine. Monk had been chosen to introduce the likes of England's Margaret Thatcher and France's François Mitterand to real North Carolina barbecue. Undaunted, he flew to Williamsburg and

NORTH CAROLINA BARBECUE : *Flavored by Time*

served the meal without a hitch. It seems that his luck continued to hold: the only out-of-town event he had ever catered before in his life was in Williamsburg, so he was already familiar with the layout. He even had a former employee who lived there and was ready to pitch in as the local liaison.

However, Monk does not consider serving his barbecue to the leaders of the world as his greatest achievement. He says that his biggest satisfaction has come in adopting one local specialty and helping to make it great, and the way he says it leaves little doubt that he *does* consider Lexington barbecue great. In addition to being utterly sold on his product, he's also become really stubborn about the way it's prepared. Monk vows that as long as he has anything to do with it, Lexington Barbecue will continue to cook with wood. While he shakes his head in mock disbelief over the number of Lexington restaurants that have switched to cooking with electricity, he acknowledges that in ten, fifteen, perhaps twenty years, all the restaurants in town may have given up on cooking over live coals because of the expense and the uncertainties of environmental regulation. "But I'm only fifty-nine," he adds. "I've got quite a few more years in me, and as long as I'm the one making the decisions, we'll continue to cook and serve our barbecue the way we always have."

Lexington Barbecue is located on the I-85 Business loop, also known as U.S. 29/70, which runs through High Point, Thomasville, and Lexington. Approaching Lexington from the north on this road, follow the signs for Charlotte, rather than bearing left to enter downtown Lexington; you'll find the restaurant on the right, with easy access via service drives. From the south, continue to follow the green I-85 Business signs; once you spot the restaurant on your left, you'll need to exit right onto a service drive, then cloverleaf under the main highway. Closed Sunday.

Alston Bridges Barbecue
Shelby

The barbecue business is so physically demanding and time consuming that the bonds of family are usually required to hold it together through the years. Today, few are willing to accept the long hours and exhausting work required to run an outstanding barbecue restaurant. Those that do usually possess a sense of continuity and pride that has been passed down through succeeding generations, as well as a direct stake in the considerable financial rewards such a business can provide. At Alston Bridges Barbecue in Shelby, a third generation is carrying on the family barbecue tradition, and in this case, it's a tradition tied directly to Warner Stamey—the man who taught virtually all of today's outstanding piedmont barbecuers their craft.

Stamey learned how to roast pork shoulders to perfection from Jess Swicegood and Sid Weaver in Lexington, where he had gone to high school in the late 1920s while living with a sister. After building up a nest egg, Stamey moved back to Shelby, his hometown, in 1930. While there, he ended up teaching his newly acquired barbecue skills to his wife's brother, Alston Bridges, as well as to Red Bridges (no relation), who would later own Bridges Barbecue Lodge, across town from Alston's place. Before long, Stamey moved back to Lexington, then later on to Greensboro, but in the 1950s, he opened a Shelby restaurant in partnership with Alston Bridges. Bridges eventually bought the site from Stamey and opened his own place in 1956.

Kent Bridges, Alston's son, was with his father from the beginning, giving him nearly forty years behind the counter at the restaurant. During that time, Kent's four children literally grew up in the business, often spending hours playing in the restaurant's basement while their father and his wife, Linda, were tending to business upstairs. Mabel Bridges, Alston's widow, taught the children to count money and make change, and she would sometimes ask to see the bills in their wallets, giving them a bonus if she found the presidents' heads turned in the same direc-

tion. As they got older, the children learned to wash dishes and do other jobs around the restaurant. Now, the reins of leadership are being handed over gradually to Jay, Reid, and Michelle, the three oldest children. They all made the decision to enter the family business full-time after exploring other career options in college. Laura, the fourth sibling, is still evaluating her future as she attends college.

Two walls of the restaurant on Grove Street are dedicated to family photographs. One wall features portraits of Alston and Mabel Bridges; the other contains the Christmas card photos of Kent and Linda Bridges, their children, and their grandchildren. In one photo, the Bridges are posing with baby pigs, while in another, they're surrounded by cows ("since we serve beef, too").

There have been some changes since the early days. Instead of coming in at midnight to get the pork shoulders on the pits so they'll be ready for the next day's lunch crowd, the third-generation Bridges now arrive early the next morning. That's because the restaurant instituted a shortened cooking process: the shoulders spend their first few hours in an electric cooker before being finished over hardwood coals on the pits. Kent and the children decided on this change together, and they all say Alston and Mabel Bridges would have applauded what the younger Bridges see as a realistic balance between the demands of

NORTH CAROLINA BARBECUE : *Flavored by Time*

work and the responsibility of spending time with their families.

In any case, customers who grew up on Alston Bridges's slow-cooked pork claim that the barbecue continues to live up to its lofty, old-time reputation. On one occasion, I ran into a couple in the parking lot who had just driven fifty miles from Morganton to Shelby for the sole purpose of enjoying a plate of Alston Bridges's barbecue, something they do several times a year. That brought to mind a moment in Joe Murphy's fine documentary on southern barbecue, *Slow Food for Fast Times*, when a customer remarked that a particular restaurant's barbecue was "a good thirty-mile barbecue," meaning he would be willing to drive that far, one way, to eat it. A fifty-mile barbecue is obviously something pretty special.

One of the main reasons customers go to such lengths to enjoy the barbecue at Alston Bridges is that the pork shoulders aren't removed from the pits until they're slow roasted to their very peak of tenderness. And tenderness is not a factor the Bridges family takes lightly. There's one particular fork, prized

The Bridges Family
Front row, left to right: Michelle, Chelsea, Julian, Whitney, Kent, and Linda
Back row, left to right: Laura, Carol, Jay, Alston, Elizabeth, Emily, and Reid

above all the others, that's almost always used to test the shoulders to see if they're done. The "magic fork," as it's known, has a bent tine and a broken shaft that's been welded together, but apparently, no other fork provides exactly the same feel. On several occasions when the fork was lost, the Bridges children have pawed through the garbage dumpster to reclaim it. Perhaps the implement is more of a superstition than anything, since the years have taught the family members to tell when a shoulder is done simply by looking at it. Still, they always reach for the magic fork. You don't toy with success.

The pit-cooked offerings at Alston Bridges are more diverse than those at most piedmont barbecue places, perhaps because the restaurant's regular customer base spreads well into the nearby Blue Ridge mountains, where an entirely different barbecue tradition has taken root and spread westward. The unofficial motto at Bridges is, "If it can be cooked on a pit, we'll cook it (within reason)," and the menu features not only the mainstay barbecued pork shoulder, but also pork ribs, beef brisket, and on certain days of the week, even chicken. However, make no mistake about it; the pork barbecue at Alston Bridges is the genuine article and should be viewed as being squarely in the center of the piedmont North Carolina tradition.

The sauce at Alston Bridges Barbecue is not overly sweet, leaning more to the peppery, spicy-vinegar side than most "dips" in this part of the state. Unlike many places, Alston Bridges's doesn't premix the sauce into the meat; instead, it is ladled over the barbecue just as it's served. The regular barbecue, which has a delicate but unmistakable wood-smoke flavor, is hand chopped, a little more finely than most. However, this is a restaurant where the staff is so accommodating that you can get the meat brought to your table just about as finely or as coarsely chopped as you like simply by asking for it. (Kent Bridges says he is constantly amazed at the inventive requests of his customers but, he shrugs, "We're here to serve barbecue—period.") They also serve a great many sandwiches containing extremely tender *slices* of barbecued pork, topped with a very finely chopped coleslaw. I think these sandwiches would be my favorite if I were dropping in on a regular basis (and I wish I were).

There are few genuine, North Carolina–style barbecue places serving racks of barbecued pork ribs that are actually pit cooked over hardwood coals, but Alston Bridges is one place that does offer them. Even though ribs are popular among North Carolinians, they're normally considered as being in a class of their own, outside the normal definition of *barbecue* (unless they're pulled from a whole, roasted pig). However, the ribs at Alston Bridges are prepared very much in the Lexington style: slow cooked for hours in an

NORTH CAROLINA BARBECUE : *Flavored by Time*

enclosed pit over hardwood coals, without first having been boiled or baked, and without being basted with sauce while they're cooking. After the ribs are removed from the pit—with the meat so tender that it's barely clinging to the bone—they're immersed for an hour or so in Boss Sauce. This sauce, a creation of Kent Bridges, has a sweeter, more complex flavor than the regular barbecue sauce, and it sets off the natural sweetness of the rib meat to perfection. These are memorable ribs, and if you're able to make only one visit to Alston Bridges's place, I strongly suggest that you either include them in your order or have them pack up a batch you can take along with you.

In North Carolina, baked beans are not a side dish that's widely served with barbecue, but at Alston Bridges Barbecue, you'd be well advised to step outside the normal coleslaw-and-hush-puppies routine to try this particular recipe. The beans simmer for several hours in a thick, tangy tomato sauce with lots of chopped bacon, onion, bell pepper, and brown sugar; and their rich, sweet flavor provides a delightful counterpoint to the wood-smoked taste of the barbecued pork.

Lunchtime, in particular, is extremely busy at Alston Bridges Barbecue. There's a glassed-in area set aside strictly for takeout orders, and on a cold day, you're liable to find yourself packed into the tiny vestibule with twenty or thirty others, like commuters on a rush-hour subway train, as you wait for your order. Meanwhile, all the seats at the counter will be full, with customers waiting two-deep behind each stool, and the dining room tables will be jam-packed as well. But the service is extremely efficient, and even at the peak periods, you probably won't have to wait longer than fifteen minutes. Whatever you do, don't get impatient and leave, because this place is well worth the wait.

The easiest directions for reaching Alston Bridges are from the U.S. 74 Bypass in Shelby. Turn north onto DeKalb Street opposite Shelby High School. Follow DeKalb Street until it dead-ends opposite the hospital and turn right on Grover Street. The restaurant is about a block-and-a-half on the right side. Closed Sunday and Monday.

Bridges Barbecue Lodge
Shelby

The first thing you'll notice when you drive up to Bridges Barbecue Lodge on the U.S. 74 Bypass just east of Shelby is that this has to be the neatest, cleanest barbecue place on the face of the earth. (Hmmmm, you might say—what about the commonly held belief that the shabbiest exterior generally houses the best barbecue?) For a moment, you think you may have stumbled into one of those all-electric, franchise barbecue places, with the calico curtains and fake country furnishings: it's all just too *nice*. The parking lot, shaded by large trees, is immaculate. There's a split-rail fence and a neat mailbox decorated with a pink pig. Then you spy the woodpile out back, which is just about as large as the restaurant. That's a good sign . . . but wait, what is it about this woodpile? The logs are neatly stacked according to length and diameter, and the whole thing looks like it's just been dusted. This is no man's woodpile, all tumbled over with the logs lying every which way. This woodpile—in fact, this restaurant—has a *woman's* touch all over it.

Bridges is still known to some folks around Shelby as Red Bridges's Barbecue, but Red's widow Lyttle—otherwise known as "Mama B"—is the heart and soul of the place. The current restaurant is actually the business's second building at this location; the first burned during the '60s. Bridges is celebrating fifty years in business, and for the last thirty of those fifty years, Mama B has steadfastly carried on the business her late husband Red originally learned from Warner Stamey in the '30s and established on his own in 1946. No doubt, Mama B and her husband both had red hair when they started out in business, but since Red's been gone since the mid '60s, she's now the only one the staff refers to as "the redhead." When I visited, the waitresses

were sporting fiftieth anniversary sweatshirts adorned with a red-headed female cartoon pig and the verse:

> "Mama B for fifty years
> Served her pork to all you dears.
> She will serve for fifty more
> The barbecue you all adore."

Lyttle's daughter, Debbie, is a striking woman who returned some twenty years ago to help her mother run the business, after spending several years as a professional model. In fact, this is a good-looking family all around. Studio photographs of Debbie's son and daughter, Chase and Natalie, are proudly displayed on the dining room walls, along with a portrait of Red Bridges, the founder, looking sharp in a fedora hat.

Debbie says that at age five and at her father's urging, she used to dance on the restaurant's tables, back when all the booths were outfitted with individual jukebox terminals. Although she no longer dances on tables, the frequent bantering between Debbie and her mother is entertainment enough for the diners who sit up front at the curved counter near the kitchen. Whether you settle onto a stool here, just inside the front door, or find a table or booth in the quiet, wood-paneled dining room, don't expect the waitress to hand you a menu. What passes for a menu at Bridges is simply a slip of paper used by the waitresses for taking orders. There are a few other items available, but the stock in trade is, of course, piedmont-style pork shoulder, slow roasted over hardwood coals and served up in either a sandwich, a barbecue tray, or a barbecue plate. Sandwiches come wrapped in aluminum foil, loaded with meat and coleslaw, and with the bun toasted crispy on top. Trays are simply a serving each of meat and slaw, plus hush puppies, while plates come with all of the above plus french fries.

The barbecue is available minced, chopped, or sliced. If you order it minced, it will be very finely chopped and mixed with a heavy dose of sauce, whereas the chopped comes chunky and laced with crusty bits of outside brown, with just a hint of sauce. The rather mild vinegar-tomato dip has the distinction of being served warm—Bridges is one of the only barbecue restaurants in the state to do this—and you'll get an extra Styrofoam cup of sauce with your order. The meat itself is some of the best I have tasted anywhere in North Carolina: moist, sweet, and incredibly tender, while still maintaining its body. I always particularly notice the grain and texture of barbecued meat—the way it bites, if you will—and Phil Schenck, the longtime pit man at Bridges, obviously knows how to get the 250 or so shoulders he cooks every week just about perfect. I believe subjecting meat that's this good to mincing can't help but diminish some of its best characteristics, so I

would recommend ordering your barbecue chopped or sliced—either of which will virtually melt in your mouth. The outside brown meat that's available by special order is as good as you'll find anywhere.

Bridges was featured in the December 1994, issue of *Gourmet* magazine after itinerant food writers Jane and Michael Stern stopped by—attracted, they said, by the number of police cars in the parking lot (which is a sign of either trouble or a very good eating spot—in this case, the latter). Of all the glowing comments in the Sterns' piece, the Bridges family and staff got the biggest kick out of a description of their coleslaw as having "a pearlescent cinnabar hue . . . a handsome complement to your pork of choice." Whew! But the Sterns are right: it is attractive slaw, with just the right crunch and sweet-tart balance to perfectly showcase the moist, rich meat.

Bridges's hush puppies are unusual. For one thing, they're a little longer and larger in diameter than the norm for this part of the state. Then too, they have a grainier texture and slightly darker color than the average Lexington-style pup, which usually comes with a rather smooth outer crust and a perfect light gold color. Let's see, maybe this is more of a shaggy, robust hush puppy—a spaniel, rather than a terrier—satisfyingly crunchy and hearty with flavor from the marriage of cornmeal and a touch of onion.

A little touch that I especially enjoyed at Bridges was the green ceramic teapot brought to the table with my order. It held enough to provide several delicious refills for my ice tea, and it was accompanied by a healthy chunk of lemon to help balance the overwhelming sweetness which barbecue lovers apparently demand in their tea.

It's obvious that Lyttle Bridges derives not only her income, but also a great deal of her social contact and her overall sense of satisfaction in life from operating the restaurant. She says the biggest challenge has been "to become the best," but unhesitatingly adds that she thinks she's achieved that with the help of her coworkers, several of whom have been with her for a long time. "I've always liked to work hard," she says, but she points out that she tries to maintain the level of excellence by providing the staff a good balance between work and rest. The restaurant is closed each Monday and Tuesday, and also closes down completely for a week in July and the week after Christmas. Of course, Mama B says she's still at the restaurant during those breaks—"lifting up everything in this restaurant and cleaning underneath it."

As a matter of fact, Mrs. Bridges wouldn't let us leave without inspecting what she proudly claims are "the cleanest floors in the barbecue business." She didn't make us eat off them to prove her point, but we probably could have. "I've been cleaning up my whole life," she sighs in mock exasperation, making it abundantly clear that she loves every minute of it. To prove it, I'm determined to catch her one day in the act of dusting that woodpile.

To reach Bridges Barbecue Lodge from Interstate 85 west of Gastonia, turn west on U.S. 74 toward Shelby. As you reach the eastern edge of Shelby, stay to the left on the bypass; you'll find Bridges Barbecue Lodge on the left side, just across U.S. 74 Bypass from the Cleveland Mall. Remember, they're closed on Monday and Tuesday.

Postscript

Barbecue obviously enjoys a high level of appreciation as a cultural symbol in North Carolina, but there's no getting around the fact that the old ways are dwindling. At some places, the veterans who have fired the pits for decades are aging, and they'll be nearly impossible to replace once they're gone. Establishments whose owners have no family members waiting in the wings are being sold, and when ownership changes, restaurants sometimes have to change from pit cooking to gas or electricity in order to get insurance coverage. Wood is becoming increasingly expensive and difficult to obtain.

And for many people, the desire to reduce fat intake makes foods like barbecue, hush puppies, and fried chicken practically off-limits.

But all is not gloomy. Traditions are being handed down from one generation to the next at some restaurants, and new blood enlivens the atmosphere at the oldest, most tradition-rich barbecue establishments. High technology and dizzying social change make us anxious to cling to cultural connectors, like barbecue, that evoke associations with family, roots, and agrarian self-sufficiency. New residents are anxious to explore and absorb the cultural characteristics of their adopted home state. Nostalgic events such as pig-cooking contests and festivals help keep barbecue and its traditional practices in the public eye. And more than ever, people want to eat in a place that has a little character and local color. As long as these trends continue, the future of barbecue seems secure.

Since barbecue is a part of our heritage that can't be preserved in a museum or a book, but must be experienced first hand, I believe a smaller, tougher band of barbecue's traditional practitioners will survive—and people will continue to beat a path to their door. As long as there are people dedicated to keeping the fires alive, there are a lot of us who will want to make sure this three-hundred-year tradition won't simply drift away and disappear . . . like smoke.

Index